SWING TRADING STRATEGIES

The Ultimate Guide on How to Make Passive Income using Options, Stocks, Forex and Commodities with profitable trades, technical analysis and mastering your emotions to win

Douglas Elder

Table of Content

INTRODUCTION

Swing trading options is a good way to make money, especially for novice traders. With this book, you will start your journey towards trading success. This trading method relies on the reactions occurring in major trends whether up or down. Swing trading has proven to be a hit for many committed Forex traders especially since the time frame ranges from 2 days to several months. The goal of being a swing trader is to identify the trend that moves up or down and then place a trade in the best position. Once you place the trade, you ride that position until you exhaust it. Many times, the swing trader utilizes many technical indicators to determine the decisions that they take. The use of technical indicators makes it easy for you to leverage the various positions that you have and opportunities. This book covers a host of indicators that you can put to use to allow you to be a successful trader. The definition of swing trading is wide, just because the strategy grabs various influences from different strategies. You can also use swing trading to further enhance your trading skills in other areas. When used the right way, swing trading strategy is ideal for traders across many markets. It is not only applicable in the Forex market but in the equity and futures market as well. In order to understand the various strategies of swing trading, you need to have the knowledge of trading – right from fundamentals to the advanced techniques. You have to understand the building blocks of successful trading and why many traders are making it big in the trade.

Who Is This Book for?

We have tried our level best to make the book ideal for a wide range of traders and readers. First, for both experienced and novice traders, we give explanations of trading strategies which are ideal for you and tell you when to use them in each scenario. The book then looks at examples that make it easy for you to understand the concepts much easier. When you use the examples, you get to apply them to many scenarios. The book, therefore, is ideal for the person that is out to understand what swing trading is all about. This can be the student looking to advance their knowledge in swing trading concepts, or a trader looking to start or advance their trading skills. You don't need to have knowledge in Trading to make sense of this book, because it introduces you gently into the concept and builds upon it step by step. Moreover, if you have just started out in trading and all the terms you come across seem pure jargon, then this is the right book to ease you into the system. Happy reading!

CHAPTER 1:
INTRODUCTION TO SWING TRADING
AND HOW IT WORKS

Swing trading represents a major short term Forex trading strategy. It works by taking advantage of the price swings in the underlying security with the aim of maximizing profits. Swing trading often lasts from a few days to two weeks and capitalizes on a security's price movement to generate income. Traders use this strategy to purchase and sell stocks whose price indicator points to an upward or downward trend in the future. They also use it to establish the momentum of stocks so as to identify the best time to trade. Because swing trading is a short-term strategy, investors must sell or buy quickly so as to increase the chance of making a profit. This trading style focuses on making smaller, but frequent incomes. It also enables buyers and sellers to cut losses as much as possible. It assumes that market prices keep changing with time and that traders can take advantage of these price movements to make money. Traders using this form of trading must always take note of the changes in the market direction and enter or exit the market as the prices swing. The main aim of swing trading is to establish and benefit from the potential of a price change. Most traders apply swing trading on stocks that have high volatility and once they make some profit from it, they exit the trade and move to the next opportunity. Swing trading is one example of aggressive trading where short-term opportunities are given priority over long-term ones. The trading style can be used on numerous financial instruments including:

- Stock

- Bonds

- Commodities

- Foreign exchange

- Stock Indices

- Cryptocurrencies

For swing trading to be effective, you must hold your trading position for some time. Since this trade capitalizes on price changes, the risk/ reward ratio is quite interesting. The trader can make a profit from each market swing and each trading period provides several opportunities to gain. Swing traders invest in a risk/ reward basis. They carry out a technical analysis of the underlying security or asset to assess how it will change in the future and then apply the available data to predict entry and leave out from trade without loss. This chapter takes an in-depth study of how swing trading works, the difference between this trade and day trading as well as other basic information you need to get started as a swing trader.

How Does Swing Trading Work?

Swing trading works using technical analysis. Because it deals with short-term trades, technical factors are used to identify opportunities. Fundamental analysis can also be incorporated to enhance returns although this is optional. For instance, a swing trader will always want to understand the fundamentals of stock that is in a bullish setup before trading. Technical analysis helps you to locate the price swings and establish whether the price will go higher or lower, depending on the trend of the charts. In doing this, you are able to restrict your investment on assets and securities that have momentum. You can also use technical analysis to take advantage of the stock's present trading pattern. Swing trading works by identifying the right time to enter trading positions. The strategy comprises of two types of swings.

- Swing low – this is when the price of a security is low

- Swing high – occurs when the price of a security is high

An investor monitors the movement of security prices between the swing low and the swing high. When the prices start rising, the trader will seek to buy from the lows and sell at the swing high. As the prices drop, the trader will sell at the swing low. Traders may miss to identify the swing low and swing high of trade but still make a profit since the strategy is based on how the price moves, not necessarily the pick positive and negative prices. For instance, long term investors may wait for six months to make a 25% profit from trade while a swing trader can make 5% profit every week. Within the six months, the swing trader would have made at least three times more than other traders. Swing traders make use of daily charts to determine the right trades. Some of the traders may also use charts with shorter time frames such as hourly and 4-hourly charts.

- The procedure for engaging swing trading is as highlighted below:

- The trader buys or sells trending security or asset after the correction or consolidation period is over

- The stock prices move up or down based on the technical analysis

- The trader then sells or buys stock, in a framework of one week, for a given rate. This percentage becomes the profit of the trade

The trader closes the current position and repeats the process again. The result of each trade depends on how well the stock price changes. Predictions vary based on the type of factors considered by the investor. This is why you may find a trader buying a stock when the majority of people are selling and selling when others are buying. This is common when there is a news release that affects pricing.

Difference between Swing and Day Trading

Day trading and swing trading usually confuse many people that wish to get into the trade. Understanding the core differences makes it possible for you to understand what each strategy stands for and how you can use it each day. The main difference between swing trading and day trading is the duration of holding a position. Day trading allows you to close a position at day end. It signifies that an investor has to buy and sell with the understanding that each trade must close by the end of the day. Most day traders engage in various asset trades within the day as a way of maximizing profits. Swing trading, on the other hand, lasts from a day to two weeks, and sometimes more. Traders do not have a restriction in times of time. One advantage of swing trading over day trading is that swing traders have more time and can make more profit. However, trade has fewer opportunities with a high probability of success. Leaving the positions open overnight also poses a great risk to swing trading investors. The price may gap down significantly and cause tremendous loss. Day traders do not leave their positions overnight. This implies that their investment is subjected to less risk as much as it involves high transaction costs. Day trading takes advantage of small changes in the price of the underlying security while swing trading works best when the price changes are significantly large. As much as swing trading offers fewer opportunities to trade, the risk per trade is lower than long-term trading because position closes are often shorter. Swing trading offers more profit opportunities than day trading. Unlike day trading, you do not need to monitor your position constantly since the trading period is quite stretched. However, you must spend some time on the trading platform so as to capture major price moves with high profits and low commission rates.

Since swing trade depends on the technical analysis of the market, it is easier to maintain losses at a minimum level using some loss reduction techniques. The trader does not have to enter positions daily. However, the business needs more understanding of the market, and a lot of patience since one trade can go for weeks.

Returns

When it comes to returns, day trading is characterized by raid compounding returns. For example, if a trader risks 0.5% of her capital on trade, she will only lose this amount if the trade goes wrong. However, if she wins, she makes a profit of one percent. This is because day trading has a 2:1 reward/ risk ratio. Assuming that the trader wins half of the 6 trades she makes in a day, she will add at least 1.5% profit to her account every day. This will grow the account and in a span of one year, she will have over 200% profit. With the swing strategy, the process of accumulating profits and losses is slower than day trading. Depending on the time period for each position, the trader may result in quicker gains or slower ones.

The Swing Trading Algorithm

There are several ways through which a swing trader can take advantage of the market swings. Some traders enter into positions before the market has indicated direction change. Others prefer to wait until the market changes direction and they are sure of the direction. Traders can enter the market on the long side when the market drops and on the short side when the market rises. Profit can be realized in both ways. The goal is always to enter the market at a point where profits can be maximized. The important factor is to identify a method that suits you as a trader and use it to make consistent gains. The swing trading algorithm allows you to make a profit from the high and low swing prices of an asset. Just like any other strategy, the algorithm allows you to purchase an asset when the prices are low and sell them when the prices go high. In order to reduce the impact of technical and fundamental analysis on the algorithm, the trade gives you selling and buying signals each time your trade is successful. Swing trading is considered as a hybrid between day trading and long-term investing. The trader must learn to buy and sell quickly albeit over a long period of time. The profits are often realized from the large movement of stock prices. This trading style becomes risky when the price starts moving sideways since there is no change in security prices.

Trading Tactics

Swing trading involves assessing chart patterns. Some of the popular charts used in this trade include:

- Cup-and-handle patterns

- Shooting stars

- Flags

- Head and shoulders patterns

- Double bottoms

- Moving average crossovers

- Triangles

These charts can be used alongside other factors to come up with a trading plan. It is always advisable that you develop a strategy or plan that gives you an edge on swing trades. Your plan should include some trade setups that help you generate income. However, you must understand that no strategy can give you 100% success. There are times that you will do everything according to plan, and still fail. However, with sound risk/ reward tactics, it is not a must that you win every time to make a profit. The more sound our risk/ reward strategy is, the fewer times you need to win in order to gain an overall profit in the trade. Swing trading can be likened to fundamental trading since, in both, the trader holds positions for a longer period of time. Most fundamental traders are swing traders since it takes several days or weeks for them to trade and make a profit.

Swing Trading Baseline

Research shows that for every market that is favorable for swing trading, liquid stocks trade either above or below a certain value known as the baseline value. Traders are able to identify this baseline using the EMA discussed above. Once they identify the baseline value, they can monitor how the stock value changes in relation to the baseline to determine whether it will head up or down. Therefore, the concern of swing traders is not making a profit in one trade or locating the perfect time to buy and sell a stock. The major concern of every trader is for the stock to hit the baseline. This is important because it confirms the direction the stock price is going to take. It, however, gets more complex when the swing assumes a higher uptrend or downtrend. The trader may wait for the stock to change direction in vain and may end up losing all the capital invested.

Capital Requirements

Trading capital often varies depending on the market. Swing traders can set the starting capital basing on the type of underlying security as well as the requirements of the position entered. To generate profits, swing traders need to do a lot in terms of acquiring knowledge. Success in swing trading is often as a result of identifying a strategy that works for you and executing this strategy continuously. Combining swing trading knowledge and a lot of practice is what makes you generate income from the trade. Remember, each day starts with different prices and different swing directions. This implies that your strategy must be applicable to the various conditions and changes within the market. For this reason, it is important to practice your strategy in varying market scenarios before using it in real trade. You can do this from a demo account to avoid risking your trading capital. One great reward of this trade is time-saving. You can still close positions after the market has closed as long as you make a profit before the trade ends. Just like other forms of trading, you are your own boss when it comes to swing trading. You work on your own and set your own time.

Swing Trading and Profits

In terms of making a profit, swing traders always want to close a position as close to the upper or lower baseline as possible. This move works for most people but poses the risk of missing some good opportunities. On a strong market, it is good to wait for the stock to reach the channel line before exiting a position since there is assured profit. A weaker market means that the directional trend is not strong enough. In this case, you should not wait for the stock to reach the channel line. This will ensure that you remain safe in case the swing does not hit the channel line. Swing trading is highly recommended for beginners. It provides great potential for making a profit and the more you advance in the trade, the more you make in terms of income. Traders do receive regular feedback on their positions after a few days to help them gain confidence.

Swing Trading Indicators

It is common for traders to purchase stock, hold onto them for the market to rise then sell them. This is how most of them make a profit. Some traders can even wait for years as they make dividends from their assets. Others are always impatient to get returns and thus exit positions as soon as they can make something small out of it. Swing trading requires a strategy. Blind trading can always result in losses. Trading indicators help you to study and understand the market before entering and closing positions. If you are new to swing trading, you must understand that these indicators may not work immediately so you will need to be patient. Nevertheless, they help you establish which move to make at what time. Swing trading indicators work well with stable markets with predictable trends. They only give you a picture of what to expect, but do not provide an accurate prediction of future markets. Here are some of the most popular indicators used to determine swing trading movements.

Exponential Moving Average

Moving averages provide traders with resistance and support levels. They also help identify bearish and bullish patterns in the market. Resistance and support levels help you to understand when to purchase a stock. Bearish and bullish patterns always indicate the points at which you should enter or exit the trade. It provides the investor with clear trading signals as well as entry and exit points. The EMA is considered better than simple moving averages because it relays these signals and points faster, giving the trader enough time to close most deals with a profit. Several trading strategies including swing trading utilizes the exponential moving average to identify trade points. A bullish crossover EMA for example; this happens every time the price moves up beyond moving average, soon after dropping from the average. This implies that there is a high possibility that a reversal may occur, or that an uptrend has just started. Whenever a nine-period EMA goes beyond a 13-period EMA the trader should make a long entry. A bearish crossover, on the other hand, takes place when the price of a stock falls below the specified EMAs. This indicates a potential decline in the market and signals the trader to plan an exit from a long trade. If the nine-period EMA falls below the 13-period EMA, the trader should make a short entry or a long exit. EMA systems are straightforward when it comes to determining the trend of swing trades. They work in combination with the right security, time frame, and swing trade fundamentals. For the EMA principle to benefit you as an investor, you must learn how to use it correctly. Most traders incorporate the EMA in their exit and entry strategies to ensure that they maximize their trading experience.

You can use moving averages to:

- Determine the trend strength – the farther away the trend and price are from the moving average, the weaker the market it. In weak markets, the price has a high potential of making a reversal.

- Establishing trend reversals using crossovers – Moving average crossovers also signal trend reversals. You need to watch out for reversing bearish or bullish trends. Be warned, however, since some crossovers tend to be fake. These always catch new traders off-guard. Always confirm a reversal using other methods and tools before closing your positions.

Relative Strength Index

This indicator also helps you find the best positions in swing trading. It gives you information that helps you determine when to enter into a trade. The indicator investigates short signals using a number of assumptions and alerts you whether the market is range-bound or flat. The RSI also gives an indication of the price strength and alerts you when a particular stock is overbought or oversold. The indicator can be combined with other factors to determine trade entries and exits. A stock is said to be oversold when its value is lower than the actual price. Most people buy the stock at this point because there is a potential of making a good profit from the price reversal. When the stock is overbought, the prices tend to go high. You should avoid such stock because there is a possibility of the prices being corrected downwards. RSI uses a security's volatility level and performance history to determine its future trend. The index is always expressed as a score ranging between 1 and 100. In a nutshell, the RIS helps you to:

- Establish oversold and overbought market conditions – this information helps you determine future corrections and reversals. Basically, overbought security signals a bearish trend correction or reversal. An oversold security signals bullish trend correction or reversal. The numbers for oversold and overbought conditions are 70/30. That is 70 overbought/ 30 oversold or 70 overvalued, 30 undervalued. Some traders use 80/20 to make room for fake outs.

- Finding divergences – RTI helps you to derive divergences which can be used to identify reversals in the swing market. Divergence is of two types: bearish and bullish. Bullish divergence is reached at whenever the price drops up to a new low, while the RSI remains the same. The bearish divergence comes into existence soon as the price moves to a high yet still maintaining the RSI. Large swings that happen so quickly result in fake-outs or false signals. This is why you need to confirm the trend using other factors before entering or exiting a swing option.

Visual Analysis

Just like any other indicators, the visual analysis indicator offers you with rich information about the swing trade market. The difference between this indicator and the rest is that the information is delivered to you in the form of a visual pattern. Visual patterns are easy to study. They make it easy for you to understand trend information.

Volume

Though ignored by most swing traders, volume indicators are also easy to understand. They provide you with information about the liquidity of securities and use this to determine the direction of the market. Traders make use of these indicators to make informed decisions in swing trading. The indicators can help you avoid emotional trading. Since swing trends keep changing each day, you need these indicators to determine the direction a trade will take. Most traders who start trading without the knowledge of these indicators take a lot of time before they can master the process and realize a profit. Most people also try working using some of these indicators then stop along the way because the indicators failed to work as expected. Some keep switching from one to another in an attempt to locate one that is easier to learn and use. It is always advisable that you identify one tool or indicator which you find easy to learn and apply it to your strategy instead of trying out all of them at once.

The Rules of Swing Trading

These are also known as the commandments of swing trading. They are used to provide guidance to traders, especially beginners. You can employ these rules if you want to grow your investment in swing trading.

1. Align your strategy with the market. The direction of the market determines how the price of a stock will be in the future. Have market trends in mind whenever you are working on your swing trading strategy. These trends should form the basis upon which you make your trading decisions. If your strategy only works for

the short-term, you may only make limited amounts of profit. Therefore, you should work with long-term trends and prepare a strategy that is able to accommodate any changes in the market conditions.

2. Short weakness. Long strength. When the market is bullish, make long trades and when the market is bearish make short trades.

3. Protect your account. If you are not sure about swing trading, you can lose money as quickly as you make it. To be on the safer side, use a practice account until you are confident enough with your trading skills. This will help you overcome the temptation of putting your capital on trades that may work against you. The rule is, never put money that you cannot afford to lose in a swing trade.

4. Identify volatile markets. Stocks that demonstrate high fluctuations in prices are the best for swing trading. The wider the price range, the higher the profit. Small price ranges generate very little profit.

5. Understand market phases. Besides swing trading trends, be sure to study the general stock market for some trends. These also give you a peek into the

direction of your swings. If the general market is bullish, upswings may be stronger and if it is bearish downswings are likely to be stronger than the upswings.

6. Understand your entry and exit points. Establish signals that give you a go-ahead into the market. You need to determine the buying time and selling the time of your orders. Use indicators to determine if a certain stock is changing direction before you buy and whether it has peaked before you make a sale. Together with this, make sure you understand the markets support and resistance ranges. These help you determine whether the swing will trend upwards, downwards or remain flat.

7. Trade on both short-term and long-term charts. The swing trading time frame features charts that define daily, weekly and even hourly patterns. To diversify your strategy, make use of all manner of charts to determine the one that gives you the most in terms of profit. In most cases, small charts involve a lot of risks. They also cost more. The best way is to analyze stock using the long-term moving average so as to determine its trend over a good period of time. You can work with

different charts at the same time and compare the results. This will help you predict the direction of certain trades both in the short-term and long-term.

8. Enter trades at the start of the trend. To make the most out of swing trades, enter positions at the beginning. The earlier you start to trade the less risky it is to make losses. This will also help you to get out of the market before stocks are oversold or overbought.

Using these rules helps you avoid impulse buying, which is common in swing trading. Although some impulses can end in profit, most of them always return losses. Establish stop-loss orders for your account, especially if you are new to the trade. This will help preserve your capital as you trade.

CHAPTER 2:
SWING TRADING MARKET CHARACTERISTICS

The main goal of swing trading is to generate income. Each trader spends time on swing trading platforms with the aim of finding a stock whose prices are bound to move over a few days or weeks and make a profit from these movements. It is the responsibility of the trader to identify such stocks on the market using research and technical analysis methodologies. When used correctly, these methodologies increase your chances of making good profits.

How to Start Swing Trading

Swing trading is not very fashionable as found in stock markets today. It could be because it is an intermediate of day and long-term trading. If you are a beginner in this kind of trade, you may need to do a number of things to get started. We look at some of this below.

1. Identify a basic strategy. Swing trading is surrounded by several simple as well as complicated strategies. If you incorporate more advanced strategies too early in the trade, you may get frustrated and overwhelmed by the entire process. As you get into the trade, you must understand that it is not easy to master all the concepts at once. Starting out on complex patterns can make you miss vital parts of your trading positions and this will only mean one thing – loss of capital.

2. Have the market trend in mind. There are several swing trading indicators that you can use to determine the direction of the market. These enable you to predict future trends and use them to maximize your profits. In case the market has an uptrend, only take the signals going the same direction. The opposite is true for markets that are moving down.

3. Be patient. In every trade, there are profits and losses. In case you lose, do not get angry. Stick by plans, strategies, and tips that reduce the risk of losing your capital. This is because the market depends on several factors and in order to succeed in the trade you must incorporate most of these factors in your trade.

4. See the big picture. Swing trading involved a combination of several tools, charts, patterns, and pointers. None of these can work alone. Therefore you should not focus on a single chart pattern, indicator or trend and believe that you will easily make a profit from it. Try out a combination of several of these.

5. Study stock patterns. As mentioned earlier, never get started until you have understood the direction that your ideal stock may assume in future. You can compare more than one trading instruments to establish any correlation between them. Avoid trading on stocks that are taking the same direction all the time since by doing this you will double your risk. There are particular types of stocks that perform better in swing trading than others. There are also times when some become too static or too volatile. You must have this in mind as you begin to trade.

6. Start with a demo account. If you are new to swing trading, it will be better if you make isolated trades first before increasing the number of positions you enter at one go. If you still have doubt about the platform you are using, start trading using a demo account just to get acquainted on the process and what is involved.

7. Trading costs. To get started, you only need a trading capital and transaction costs. For most platforms, you can easily start swing trading with as little as $5000.

In summary, swing trading basically involves getting the right market and the right stock. The best traders normally select stocks that have high fluctuation rates because these result in huge profits. As a beginner, however, you should focus on markets that possess less risk and shorter trading periods. As time goes by, you can increase the trading periods significantly since you will be able to manage the risks involved. In case you need to make higher profits within a short period of time, you may consider trading in stocks that belong to large companies. These are often known as large-cap stocks and are always on high demand because of the high returns.

Swing Trading Terminology

Several terms are used in swing trading. As a trader, you must understand what each of these terms refers to for you to trade successfully. Let us look at some of the popular ones.

- Bid: the best price or offer to purchase a certain stock or security

- Candlestick: a charting method used by traders to predict price changes in a swing market. Candlestick patterns can also help you identify swing low and high points in trade charts.

- Downtrend: A state when the price of a stock or security is on the decline. EMA: This stands for the exponential moving average. It is one of the strategies used in swing trading.

- Pullback or retrace: A non-dominant occurrence where the price of a stock moves in the same direction as the market trend.

- SMA: An abbreviation of a simple moving average. This is also a strategy in swing trading.

- Trendline: A line used to define the trend of a particular stock on the price chart.

- Uptrend: A state where the price makes more highs than lows

- Volume: Refers to the number of shares trader for each stock item over a period of time.

Swing trading is one of the techniques that allow you to hold onto a stock for some time before releasing it. The prices are often determined intra-weekly or intra-monthly.

The Swing Market and Large-Cap Stocks

Large-cap stocks are always on high demand when it comes to swing trading. Most of these stocks belong to fortune 500 companies that have a history of good prices and favorable trading terms. Swing traders take advantage of these stocks because they feature large price fluctuation ranges that translate to big profits. Since the changes in pricing occur within short time spans, traders make quick profits from this both in bullish and bearish markets. Most companies that feature large stocks are also the best when it comes to chief exchanges.

Swing Trading Markets

Generally, swing trading operates in two market types: the bull market and the bear market. If you find yourself in between these two trades then you are at the right position to swing trade. Swing trading works best in markets that begin well at position entry, decline for some time then rise again as the trading period ends. As a trader, you must understand which trades to make during bearish and bullish periods. An ideal swing trading environment is where market prices are not moving at all. During a bearish or bullish market, the momentum always carries stock in the same direction for a long period of time. Just like long-term trading, the success of swing trading is often based on how correct the trader identifies the current type of market. Most markets change very little as time goes by. Some do change in a few days; decline for more days then rises again. Small swings happen more often than big ones. By the end of the trading period, the market would have made several upward and downward shifts. The main essence of swing trading is capturing some profits from these small yet frequent swings. Swing traders should select trades from stock that is active, and one that has a tendency to swing in well-defined patterns.

Counter Trending Swing Trading

Counter trending refers to the process of making a profit from the frequency at which swing trends break down. As noted earlier, each time you spot increased highs in a swing trading chart then there is likely going to be a continuous uptrend on the market. More decreasing lows signify a downtrend on the market. Most markets start high and then are followed by retracement periods before stabilizing. A counter-trend seeks to make a profit from the retracement or reverse period. In this case, the trader monitors an uptrend pattern than when the line reaches a new high and starts to break; he buys stock in anticipation that the price will reverse direction. When it comes to counter trending, the trader must maintain a high state of discipline so that the prices do not work against him. If the market assumes a trend that can make you lose, you must decide whether to exit the position or give it some more time. You must, however, bear in mind that if the trend does not break again you may lose a lot of money.

Swing Trading Systems and Software

This refers to programs that help you to leverage your trading strategies by making it easy for you to establish market trends and other important features. They identify trading opportunities on your behalf, saving you time and resources. Some of the best software programs make suggestions on the type of stocks that you need to trade in and alert you when to buy or sell at a profit. Trading systems often take the form of charts. They help you to identify trends in the marketplaces and make winning trades. If you have been into swing trading for some time now, you agree that predicting stock prices manually from historical trends is not easy. This is where trading systems and programs come in. the systems utilize oscillations to obtain information on the stock prices. Traders who utilize such systems in their transactions can easily leverage on short-term stock price changes without fearing about competition from other investors. Swing trading systems are not meant for everyone. They are mostly used by part-time traders who do not have enough time to enter market positions and monitor price changes all the time. Some of these traders only get to check the market once in a day or even week and therefore rely on information released by brokers. Expert traders can also use trading systems once in a while to make small profits. One downside of these systems is that they only work in stable market environments. This is because such markets only make small changes in prices that can be easily ignored. However, a good system is capable to make good profits from these changes. The systems do not work well in bearish and bullish markets because the price only moves in one direction instead of fluctuating. As a trader, you must, however, test any system to ascertain that it works before using it on your real trading account. Typically, swing trading markets change in four phases.

- Phase one is where the market is bound by a certain range. The price oscillates between two boundaries and these are treated as the upper and lower boundary for the trade. Simple systems make money from this by initiating a long position at the upper boundary and a short position at the lower boundary.

- Phase two is where the price goes beyond the upper boundary and stabilizes into a trend. The price then continues to rise and fall alternatively until the peak swing is reached. This results in another trading range and can be considered as phase 3.

- During the last phase, the price drops from phase three and goes below the trend.

Most trading systems take this into account when creating positions. A good system is always capable of detecting whether the market is within a bound range or if it has started trending. Some systems work well when the market is trending but are useless when the range is bound. This is why you must test a system's feature before using it for your swing trades.

Swing Trading Plan

Just like a trading system, a system trading plan helps you manage your trades. Having well-defined objectives and possible outcomes of a trade are very essential when it comes to swing trading. A trading plan ensures that you remain consistent in your trading routine. It removes any guesswork that comes with not having a strategy. Discipline is what makes every successful trader. A sound plan also helps you to analyze and adjust your trading history and strategy in a way that minimizes loss. Depending on the outcome of your trades, you can easily tell if your plan is effective or not. The plan keeps you away from outside interference as you set to understand the right times to trade. One item that must appear in your plan is the study of swing charts. These are graphic figures that represent changes in the price movement of certain stocks. Swing charts are often easy to understand because they eliminate the noise found in bar charts. With swing charts, it is easy to identify features like:

- Support and resistance levels

- Swing highs and swing lows

- Chart patterns

- Channel areas

- Stock strength

Traders can use each swing high and low on these charts as a trendline. Each chart features several meaningful points including flags, pennants, double tops, double bottoms among others. These are often straightforward in swing charts. It is also easier to apply tools such as trend lines, retracements and extensions on swing charts than it is for any other charts.

Trading Routines

Unlike other forms of trading, swing trading utilizes both technical and fundamental analysis to track price movements and establish momentum. Using this type of routine helps raise higher returns from a very small capital. The downside of this is that the process involves high commissions and volatility. In addition to plans and routines, swing traders must be willing to learn all the time. Most trading experts have an upper hand over starters because they are more experienced and enjoy lower commissions. They have enough information about the trade and make use of it to make consistent profits. Let us look at how a typical swing trading routine should look like.

- Pre-market – most retail swing traders begin their day at 6:00 am or just before the opening bell sounds. The reason for starting early is to study the market and determine how the day is going to be. The first task should be catching up on the latest development and news on the market as these affect stock prices in some way. In terms of news, you should keep an eye on the following three items:

- The overall market sentiments including economic reports, inflation reports, currency performance and whether the market is bullish or bearish

- Industry or sector sentiments

- Current holdings in terms of the earnings, filings, etc.

- Finding potential trades – From studying the markets, the trader should then identify potential trades for that day. On many occasions, swing traders get into the market by carrying out fundamental analysis then exit the market by the help of technical analysis. Fundamental catalysts comprise of special opportunities in the industry as well as some sector plays. Special opportunities are often highlighted in daily financial news and include factors such as mergers and acquisitions, bankruptcies, restructurings, and other related ones. Most of these opportunities represent the risk you may face during the day but also deliver great rewards if researched carefully. Sector plays can be found on reputable websites that provide financial information. For instance, you can predict the trends in the energy sector by checking out popular energy news sites.

- Getting a watch list – next is to make a watch list for some of the promising stocks for that day. These should be stocks that seem to be in trade and also possess a good trend. These are always listed on your trading platform's dashboard with their various entry prices, stop-loss prices as well as target prices.

- Assess existing positions – the final step involves reviewing any of your existing positions. Check the news and trends related to these positions to ensure that your capital remained intact throughout the night. You can obtain this news by simply typing the stock's symbol on a news portal such as Google or Yahoo News. If there is any viable information on these platforms then you should study it to find out if it will affect your current positions in any way.

Market Hours

Market hours refer to the time you spent watching the market and trading in the stock. Expert swing traders utilize level II quotes to determine which investors are buying and selling which items and at what prices. As soon as an ideal market has been identified and entered, the trader begins to analyze trends so as to define an exit point. This is always done using technical analysis techniques like Fibonacci extensions as well as common resistance and support levels. Entering a trade-in swing trading is not a simple process. The timing depends on the activities of the day. However, the process of trading and exiting is often easier since most of the guidelines are pre-determined. Very few traders make use of after-hours to place trades. This is because, at such times, the market is always illiquid and further spread. An important thing to do at this time is to evaluate the trade's performance. It is always recommended that traders record all the transactions they engage in not just for performance evaluation purposes but also for tax calculations. The performance evaluation process always entails scanning through a trade's activities and identifying areas that need improvement. From this routine, you learn how important the pre-market routine is important for your trading success. It is at this time that most trading opportunities are identified and scheduled accordingly. Market hours should only be set aside for entering and exiting positions and not for planning. After hours, on the other hand, should be set aside for evaluation and taxation. Applying this routine to your trading plan can help improve your trading experience significantly. If you combine this with good trading resources and tools, you will easily make a good income from swing trading. Without a good plan, software, and routine, swing trading can be a difficult trade to master. Regardless of the market or type of stock that you trade-in, you must create a plan and routine that minimizes the risks involved, and maximizes the reward. Swing trading is one of the techniques that stands out from the crowd. Although it is neither focused on long-term trading nor on day-trading, it can yield good returns if you take time and understand every underlying concept involved in the trade.

CHAPTER 3:

THE BASICS OF INTRADAY TRADING

Intraday trades occur within one day. In stock trading, the term intraday is used to refer to stocks and EFTs that trade within normal business hours. Intraday traders take particular interest in price changes during the day and use them to make one or several trades. The value of each security fluctuates in the course of the day. Intraday figures capture these fluctuations by each hour. These figures are then used to derive high/ low price spreads for each security per day. Intraday also refers to any new highs and lows reached by certain security. For instance, a new intraday high denotes that the security in question has hit a new high in relation to other prices reached during the trading period. Most traders treat the intraday high as the closing price of a particular security. They monitor price movements using trading charts which are able to capture even the slightest fluctuation in security prices. Intraday traders mostly use 1, 5, 15, 30 and 60-minute charts to predict market trends. A good number of traders also use the VWAP or volume-weighted average price orders to increase the efficiency of trades and take advantage of price movements.

How Intraday Trading Works

In this style of trading, investors depend heavily on market volatility. Most of the stocks used are those whose prices change a lot in the course of the day. These changes are caused by a number of factors including company news, investor sentiments and earning reports. Traders also prefer stock whose liquidity is high because they are able to change trading positions even when there are no changes in the stock prices. When the price goes up the trader enters a buy position and if the price reduces, the trader may short sell in order to make a profit. Intraday trading is almost similar to day trading which involves trading in financial instruments within a day. It is one of the most preferred trading styles by most investors because they are able to close positions before the day ends. By this, any trader that wants to buy or sells must do so before the market period ends. To get started in intraday trading, you must first own a trading account. You also must specify that the orders you are placing through your account are for intraday trading so that they are automatically closed at the end of the day in case you do not do this by yourself.

Chart: Trading Intraday

Advantages

There are several benefits involved in intraday trading. A good number of traders find the trading style attractive due to the low charges levied by stockbrokers. These charges are often less than what traders pay in regular trading platforms. Another benefit of intraday trading is that traders are able to get high-profit margins within the day by transacting several times. Intraday trading does not last to the night. This means that stock prices will not be affected by external factors. There is very little possibility for the stock value to be affected by overnight factors such as economic news or broker downgrades and upgrades. Traders often look for faster exits from the market as soon as they have obtained maximum profits. Some do exit the markets within a few minutes while others trade the entire day. Investors who use intraday

43

trading to make money also benefit from the tight stop-loss orders. This ensures that the stop price is high enough to reduce losses in positions and that it is low enough for the same to happen in short positions. However, a number of disadvantages are also associated with this kind of trade. The most obvious one is the issue of time. There is always insufficient time for trading positions to realize maximum profits. Some traders do not realize any profits at all, yet must pay the commissions associated with each trade. This makes the trade quite risky for learners who do not understand how to take advantage of the price fluctuations. Starters are always advised to invest an amount they can afford to lose since there is a high possibility of not getting any income.

Choosing Stocks for Intraday Trading

Intraday traders generate income through exploiting minor price fluctuations in stocks, options, currencies, and futures. When selecting the securities or stocks to trade in, there are several factors that you must consider to ensure that your intraday trading positions bear a positive end. Here are some of them.

Liquidity

Stocks with high liquidity also have big volumes. This means that large amounts of the stock can be traded without affecting its price. Intraday trading depends a lot on timing and speed, and stocks that have large volumes makes the trade a lot easier. The depth of stock shows you how liquid stock can get at different price levels. You can tell the liquidity of a price by getting the disparity in the prices of the bid and the ask of a given security or else the gap between the real and probable value of the security. A security's volume can be defined as the frequency at which a given stock is sold or bought in a particular time frame. In intraday trading, this is also called the average daily trading stock. A stock with high volume has the potential for more profits and an increase in the volume can result in rapid changes in the stock price either upwards or downwards. Purchasing stocks that have low volume means that you will be required to hold on the stock for longer periods since it is not in demand. As you hold on the stocks, the direction of the market may change drastically and you will end up losing most of your investment.

Stock Volatility

As discussed earlier, intraday traders rely on price movements to make money. Stocks that move a lot in percentage or dollar terms are promising when it comes to returns. Most stocks change by at least 3% or $1.50 each day. Such is considered to be highly volatile. In simple terms, volatility measures the daily range in stock prices. More volatility translates to higher profits or losses.

Group Followers

A good stock to trade-in is one whose price changes are parallel to its index and sector group. This implies that when the sector and index increases, the stock price automatically goes up. This feature is important for traders who wish to buy and sell the weakest or strongest securities.

Stock Trends

One important aspect that you must analyze when choosing stock for intraday business is its trend. There are stocks that follow the general market trend. These are more predictable and can easily give you profit. There are other stocks that bear independent trends. These are often represented as wavy lines on trading charts. You will need to study these waves to determine the uptrend and downtrends. You should be able to spot new price peaks and use them to define the direction of your trades. Most traders avoid unpredictable stocks since they do not have any defined pattern that you can use to determine the course of the market.

Stock Indices

There are particular stocks that follow trends of major indices on the market. As the indices go up, the stock price also goes up and vice versa. Such stocks are easy to trade since their future prices are easily predictable. Depending on the market of such stocks, the prices may greatly be affected by world news. Therefore you must watch out for such news before initiating trade positions.

Once you have understood how to select the right securities for intraday trading, you will need to know how to establish entry and exit points to ensure that you start and close positions at the right time. Some of the tools that can help you achieve this include:

- Level 2 or ECN quotes. ECN stands for electromagnetic communication networks. The term refers to a system that makes the best ask and bid quotes for each market available to you. This information is often a collection of quotes from several traders. ECN systems also help match and execute your orders based on these quotes. Level 2 service is often subscription-based. It grants you access to some company order books that contain stock price quotes from top market traders.

- News services. Real-time news can serve as a basis to determine when you should enter a market. This is because financial news always gives you an idea of what to expect in terms of stock price changes. It is important that you subscribe to a news channel that alerts you when there are changes in your trading sector.

- Candlestick charts. These provide you with a detailed analysis of a stock's price action. Traders use the above tools to create a plan and determine when to enter a position. When it comes to intraday trading, making a purchase on the market's uptrend does not guarantee profits. More specific trading strategies recommend that you enter a short position when the price goes beyond the trendline of a particular chart.

There are several other ways that you can use to determine when to exit a long position in intraday trading. These include profit targets as well as trailing stops. Some of the strategies you can use to determine profit targets include:

- Scalping, which involves closing a long position as soon as the trade generates a profit. In this case, the profit target is the discrepancy in the existing price and the actual stock price.

- Fading. This involves buying of stock soon after its price rises suddenly. The sudden change creates an assumption that the stock has been overbought. The target is to wait for a while until the buyers step in, then you can sell your stocks at a profit. This strategy is very risky but when used correctly can be very rewarding.

- Momentum. This refers to trading that is based on news releases or trends. It is common in high volume stocks. Momentum traders buy the stock at news release and wait for the price to show signs of reversal before selling it off.

- Current turn around. This is trading based on a stock's instability. The trader purchases stock at the lowest price of the day and sells it at the highest price for that day. In this case, the price target is the point when the price shows signs of reversal. Intraday trading requires a lot of learning and practice. Before you start trading, you must understand that some of the people you will be trading against are professionals who utilize the best strategies, technologies, and connections in their transactions. Therefore you must do your homework before entering any position to avoid trading blindly. If you can successfully predict price changes in certain stocks, you can be confident that the trade will work in your favor.

Let us now look at some of the intraday trading strategies that can help you achieve more in times of planning, the timing of trades and generating returns.

Trade with the Current Trend

The stock market often moves in waves. It is upon you as a trader to understand the meaning of these waves. To make a profit in intraday trades, enter long positions during the market's uptrend and take short positions on its downtrend. This is because most intraday market trends tend to change course too often but you can still make a few trades before this happens. Determining market trends is not easy, that is why you need to use trendlines to identify entry and stop positions. Most intraday traders make a profit from equities and stocks that have high to moderate correlation with NASDAQ or S&P 500 indexes. They are then able to select a particular stock based on how strong or weak it is, based on these indexes. This provides great opportunities for traders since the price of a strong stock may change by 2% in case of the related index rises by 1%. When these indexes move up, you should purchase stocks that are also increasing in price. This is because the price of the stock may remain intact when the index pulls back, giving you high-profit potential. As the index prices drop, you can short sell stocks that are also declining in price. As the index prices keep moving in the downtrend, the price of a weak stock will not change much and this will also give you a high-profit potential from the declining market.

Work with Pullbacks

Trendlines act as boundaries within which price waves begin and end. When choosing stocks for trading, you can use trendlines to determine how early you can enter into a market. To enter a long position, make a purchase soon after the price declines towards the trendline. Do the same when entering a short-selling position as the market assumes a downward trend. Waiting for pullbacks lowers the risk of entering in a position. This allows you to make purchases and sales as close to the stop-loss level, minimizing any losses. Most traders and investors make orders only when intraday markets unlock every morning. Having many orders at the same time can result in price volatility and only professional traders can be able to make the right price predictions at this point. For a new trader, it is good to take time each morning and study the market for about half an hour before making any move. Beginners can also make more trades during the middle hours of the day because this is the time when stocks are more stable and less volatile.

Regular Trades, Regular Profits

When it comes to intraday trading, you must take advantage of the limited time available to make as many trades and as many profits as you can. Every trader must be careful not to spend a lot of time on trades that are going the wrong direction as these will always end in a loss. When trading with trends, you can take profits when the stock price is slightly higher than the former price for a long position. For the short or downward position, you may take profits at a price that is slightly lower than the former price.

Stagnant Markets

Stock prices may stall on some days. In some cases, market trends keep reversing the direction that you cannot establish the exact direction. If you spot a market that is not making any major highs and lows, do not start any trade. This is because the movements may not be large enough to yield a reward. Alternatively, you can engage a range-bound trading strategy at this point. This strategy allows you to use lines to determine a range within which you can define resistance and support areas. You can then short-sell when the price goes beyond the horizontal line and starts to decline again. Wait for the price to move to the lower part of the range for you to exit a short position. If you intend to place a stop-loss order on the trade, put it right below the most recent low price or just above the latest high price. Some traders find it difficult to alternate between range and trend trading. If you wish to engage in trend trading alone, you can step aside when the markets are in the range state. If you want to range trade, you can avoid stocks that tend to trend most of the time and concentrate on stocks that range most of the time.

Set Aside Capital and Time

For every intraday trade you engage in, find out how much you are willing to risk in case the market assumes the wrong direction. Most traders risk at most 2% of their capital in each trade. For example, if a trader has $40,000 in an account, willing to risk about 0.5% of this on every trade, he will receive$40,000 x 0.005 as the highest loss. This amounts to $200. It is important to set aside the amount of money that you are willing to lose for each trade although there is a likelihood that you will make a profit instead. Since intraday trading requires most of your time, you may need to give up most of your daily activities since you must enter and close trades in good time. If you do not have enough time to engage in this kind of trade, then don't do it. This is because intraday traders must spend a lot of time tracking the market, sealing opportunities and completing trades. The trade revolves around time.

Begin Small

One great advantage of intraday trading is that you can start with as little as one trade in a day and keep growing as you master the business. You can also focus on one type of stock first and keep adding these with time. Fractional shares are becoming a common feature in stock trading. These allow you to invest smaller amounts in trades such as this one. For instance, if a company is selling its shares at $250, you can purchase a fraction of the shares by, say $50. Look for deals that allow you to make small deposits, but keep off penny stocks. These always feature low liquidity and offer very slim chances of making a profit. Most of the stocks that trade below $5 per share are always removed from stock exchange markets and can only trade effectively over the counter. Unless you are sure of making some cash from such stocks, it is good to avoid them.

Use Stop Orders to Limit Losses

Before entering a trade, ensure you define the type of orders you will use. These could be limit orders as well as market tips not forgetting 'stop-loss' orders. For the case of Market orders, they need to be processed at the best price available for the underlying security. This means that the price for such orders is not predetermined and therefore you cannot estimate the amount of profit you will get from such trades. Limit orders help you to trade more accurately because the stock price is known. Besides these strategies, you must understand the place of information in intraday trading. Besides knowing the basic trading process, you need to stay up to date with the latest events and news in the stock sector. You must do your research and homework for each stock that you wish to make a profit from.

CHAPTER 4:
SWING TRADING STRATEGIES AND TECHNIQUES

Swing trading is one of the popular methods of making money in the stock market. It is one of the methods that allow you to maximize profits while minimizing risks. The priority of every stock market investor is to enter and exit a trade early enough. Traders achieve this by selling when the price indicates a decline and buying when the prices have the possibility of going higher. Swing trading is one of the best trading styles since it provides you with numerous trading strategies. However, the basic strategy you need to succeed in the market is to incorporate the necessary factors in determining the kind of trade that can give you profit. One of these factors is the type of market or instrument you want to trade-in. This may be stock, commodities, currencies or any other financial tool. Whatever instrument you select should be one that has the potential to trend in the future. Since market swings have a place in determining the trading style you use, you must be able to identify the right market which flows naturally and in a smooth way. Every stock

1

market behaves differently at different times. Some may be stagnant in terms of price change, while others may be too volatile. This is where swing trading strategies come in. These strategies are designed to help you improve your trading experience and results. They increase your returns and help you maximize returns. There are several strategies used in swing trading. They are useful stocks trading. Here, we summarize some of the most common strategies used by most investors. You can use these strategies to identify opportunities as well as manage your trades.

Swing Strategy 1: Fibonacci Retracement

This strategy assists you to identify support and resistance levels of your trade. These levels determine whether there is a possibility of price reversal on a particular stock. In most trades, the stock will backtrack for some time before reversing. Plotting this on a Fibonacci chart will help you determine some reverse points. As a trader, you can use these points to determine when to enter a buy or sell position. If the strategy predicts a downtrend in the prices then you can invest in a short-term sell position. This will ensure that you exit the position with a profit. Founded by Leonardo Fibonacci, this strategy is useful in identifying reversals on the stock chart. It works using an array of numbers that are added together to come up with a sequence. For example 1, 2, 3, 5, 8, 13, 21 is a Fibonacci sequence. Two previous numbers are added together to get the next in the sequence. The relationship between these numbers represents a retracement pattern that can be used to analyses stock. The strategy works on the assumption that the value of the stock will always retrace by a certain percentage before changing direction. It is believed that the retracements take place at three percentage levels – 38.2, 50 and 61.8. This is indicated in the diagram below.

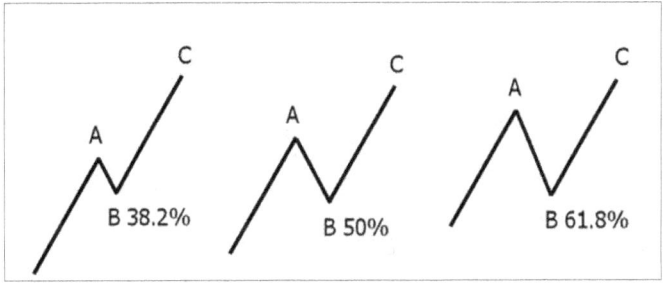

Figure 1.0 Fibonacci retracement

The above picture indicates potential reversal points for a stock whose price is rising. For a stock that is in the downward trend, the patters will face the reverse direction. When a stock is moving up, it will reach point A then retrace to part B before rising higher until it reaches part C. These swings are most useful when determining whether and when to enter into short or long positions. As the stock retraces, you can plot the points on a chart to establish the possibility of a reversal. For accurate results, you must plot the points at all the three percentage levels. Once you are done plotting the retracement points, you will need to use them to draw the Fibonacci grid. Start with the swing point highs and lows of the swing. Most charting software provides you with a tool for doing this. If the software you are using doesn't have such a tool, you can use calculate this manually by: First, calculate the difference between the high point and low point of the swing. Multiply the resultant figure with each percentage level Subtract the result from the swing point high. This becomes our Fibonacci. Below is an example of a Fibonacci grid formulated from high and low swing points.

Figure 2.0: Fibonacci Grid

4

As you draw the grid, you will realize that each line features support and resistance areas that are easy to identify. The fib grid helps you to visualize the retracement levels better. One feature of this strategy that you should know about is that it works well with trending stock markets. The idea is always to buy a stock when there is a power at the management point, and at the stable market. The trader sells the stock when there is a retracement at the resistance level and when the market is on the decline. To get the retracement levels, you must first establish a trade's highs and lows. For a downtrend, focus your attention to the highest point as you move the line towards the most recent low so as to create the levels. For an upward trend, move along the low position as you draw the line to the hottest swing high. The Fibonacci retracement swing trading strategy has several advantages. Let us look at some of them. The strategy utilizes very few trading indicators. It is therefore easy to use. Stock reversals offer safe entry into swing trades Works on trends H4 chart trading creates a balance between short and long term trends. Compatibility of the strategy with Heiken Ashi candles makes it easy to determine clear trends Every strategy has its own advantages and disadvantages. One downside of the Fibonacci retracement strategy is that price movements are often slow. It may take several days or weeks for you to hit your profit targets. The strategy is therefore not ideal for traders who need quick returns.

Swing Strategy 2: Support and Resistance Lines

This strategy is common in trading platforms that utilize technical analysis to study the market. The support level refers to an area on the swing trading chart whose value is less than the current market price. It is at this point that the prices stop going down. It occurs at the time when the buyer perceives a potential profit and purchases a stock. The purchase causes the price to stop moving down. The resistance level is an area that is above the current market price on the chart where the buying pressure can be overcome by the selling pressure. At this point, the trader can sell a position at a profit. Resistance levels act as ceilings for swing trading and occur when a seller perceives a potential for making a profit. The seller enters into a short position, overcoming the buyers. This causes the price to stop going up and instead start to move downwards. The only difference between resistance and support is that resistance occurs above the market price. Otherwise, the two concepts operate using the same concept. One thing you should note about this strategy is that each time the price goes beyond the support or resistance area, the two switch positions – the support area becomes the resistance area and vice versa. This strategy helps traders to take advantage of the changes in the support as well as in resistance stages. It could be useful in determining the end to an old trend being the start of a new one. The strategy also helps you to manage risks. For a trader to make a profit from this strategy, they must know how to identify the resistance and support levels. With the right knowledge, these are often easy to identify and using charts makes it easier. In addition to identifying these points, charts can be useful in identifying the purchasing and selling signals as well as set price targets for your swing trade positions. Support levels, as well as resistance, are highly dependent on demand and supply of the stocks. Demand and supply do affect the movement of stock prices. The stock market often goes up when demand is more than supply and declines when the opposite is true. As demand rises, prices go up. The support level occurs when demand is higher than supply. At this point, the price rises. The resistance level occurs when supply is more than demand. This results in a price fall. As a trader, you must understand that support and resistance are not clear figures but areas that represent a range of stock prices. Technical analysts often draw lines around these areas for the purposes of clarity and convenience.

Swing Highs and Lows

These highlight points where the market is scheduled to change direction or reverse. Swing highs and lows form the basis of charting resistance and support levels. Each swing point has the potential of becoming a support or resistance level. These levels can also be derived from values such as the moving average.

Swing Strategy 3: Channel Trading

This strategy allows you to locate stocks that have a strong trend and trade with them. If you identify a channel that has a bearish trend, you will be required to enter a sell position as the price goes below the channel's top line. Channels work with trends; therefore it is important that you trade with trends in mind. You only stop trading this position when the price breaks out and the prices start going up. Most people overlook this strategy despite the fact that is one of the most reliable chart patterns. Channel trading utilizes different forms of technical analysis to give you precise entry and exit points for every trade. It also helps you manage risk. As a trader, you must know how to identify channels, when to start and stop trading as well as when to place stop-loss orders in the trading process.

Characteristics of Channels

By definition, a channel refers to the state when the price of a stock or asset remains between two trend lines that are parallel to each other. The upper line connects the price to the swing high and the lower line connects the price to the swing low. When the price goes beyond cannel requirements, it indicates that more purchases are on the way. If it falls below the lower trendline, it means that more selling could be taking place. Channel trading works best with stocks that have medium volatility. By now, you probably understand the place of volatility in swing trading. If a stock or security has little volatility, the channel range will be small resulting in small profits. Large volatility translates to bigger channel ranges and larger profits.

Identifying Channels

Every trader must identify a channel before trading in it. A basic channel is made of four contact points – two lows that connect to each other, and two highs also connecting to each other. You can locate channels in three ways:

1. Manual identification – involves scanning the charts to manually locate the channel patterns. With this

method, traders trade the channels as they identify them.

2. Software identification – this is where software or application is used to automatically chart channel areas and patterns

3. Use of third parties – there are companies that offer channel identification services. You can work with such companies to get a list of equities where channel trading applies.

Generally, channels are of three types. Channels that are uprising are known as ascending channels while those that are angled downward are called descending channels. These two are also referred to as trend channels since the stock price is always moving in one direction. There are also the horizontal channels. These are channels whose prices move neither upwards nor downwards. The figure below indicates how these three channels are represented in a chart.

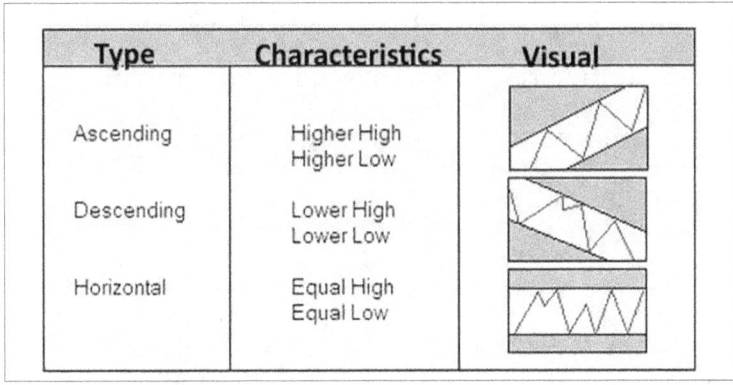

Type	Characteristics	Visual
Ascending	Higher High Higher Low	
Descending	Lower High Lower Low	
Horizontal	Equal High Equal Low	

Figure 3.0. Types of channels

Each swing trading channel has buy and sell points and for each trade, there are rules that apply. Below are some of the rules used in buying and selling swing positions:

1. As the price hits the top trendline, the trader should either sell an existing long position or enter a short position to make profit

2. When prices are in between the trendlines, do nothing. If you have no open positions do not enter any and if there exists some that are open already, do not close them.

3. Once the stock price reaches the lower trendline, cover your short positions and open a long position.

These rules work for most trades. However, there is an exception. If the price goes beyond the top or bottom channel lines then the channel is no longer viable. At this point, you should not initiate any trades until you spot a new channel. If the stock price remains within a certain range for a long time then a new narrow channel may arise. When this happens, you can enter or exit the channel using the trendlines of the narrower channels. If the channel rises, make purchases near the bottom trendline and exit these at the top trendline. If the channel is falling, make purchases near the top trendline and exit near the bottom line. To enhance the accuracy of this strategy, you may combine it with other technical factors such as candlestick patterns and swing volumes.

Swing Strategy 4: The concept of 'Moving-Average'

It is the most popular swing trading strategy. It is also the easiest. Basically, there are two types. Simple 'moving-average' as well as the 'exponential-moving-average. These two, account for the averages of given market detail composed over a certain period. The difference between the two is in terms of their speed. The exponential moving average works faster and changes direction earlier than the simple moving average. The EMA allows you more time to enter and exit swing positions than the SMA since it helps you recognize price changes in good time. Since the EMA reacts faster than the SMA, it is the most vulnerable when it comes to giving the wrong signals. The SMA is not as quick as the EMA but keeps you in trade positions longer. This allows you enough time to detect and avoid any premature and false signals. Since swing trading is a short-term style of investment, you should get a moving average that works faster and displays price changes in real-time. That is why most traders use the EMA method when using this strategy. Moving averages can also be differentiated using three different time periods. The 9 or 10 period is the most popular. It involves very quick signals and is often used for directional filtering. The 21 periods is considered the most accurate. It is common in riding trends and can be used in medium-term trading that takes a few weeks to months. The 50 period moving average is for long-term trades. It is best suited for swing trades that mature after a long time. You can also consider using larger moving averages like the 100 periods and 200/250 period. The 100 period is commonly used in identifying support and resistance levels in daily and weekly swing trades. The 200/250 period is popular for daily trades since it covers a whole year or 250 trading days.

Golden Cross and Death Cross Signals

Swing traders can use moving averages to represent directional filters. This is where the above signals come in. These two occur when 50 and 200-period moving averages meet or cross. They are used in daily charts to predict stock market trends. The Golden cross-refers to a pattern that has a bullish signal. It happens whenever the later goes beyond the former averages. In other words, it is the getaway pattern formed whenever the short-term average of security, passes over its durable average. Therefore, it is characterized by high volumes of trade and can be divided into three stages as follows:

1. Stage 1: the downtrend bottoms out and selling is closed

2. The short moving average rises to form a crossover on the larger average. This causes a breakout, resulting in a reversed trend

3. The short moving average continues rising until high prices are reached.

One limitation of the golden cross is that all its indicators are always delayed. This means that you cannot rely on them fully to predict future trends. In most cases golden cross signals are false. If you are a swing trade, you must always use other means to confirm golden cross signals to avoid getting into trouble. The accuracy of this method can be increased by using the right indicators and additional filters when confirming the signals When this crossover starts to fade, a death cross will form. The death cross is the exact opposite of the golden cross. It always indicates a high potential of a selloff and occurs when the SMA of a particular stock falls below its long-term moving average. Common moving averages that use this concept are the 200 and 50-period averages. This signal is one of the most reliable when it comes to predicting bear markets. It helps traders avoid big losses in their swing positions. Any time you spot a death cross in your swing charts, you must prepare for a bear turn in the market. However, just like the golden cross, the death cross also delays signals and must be combined with other technical factors for accurate results. Each of these signals has two lines. For a crossover to occur, one line must move faster than the other. The moving average crossover indicator is valid if the following rules apply:

- The moving average convergence/ divergence or MACD must overlap or cross

- The trader should put a sell or buy stop order based on the market trend

- The stop loss should be placed a bit far from the trade entry point to avoid premature stops

- When exiting a trade, wait for the signal to change direction. For instance, if you had open a buy position, wait for a sell signal before exiting the trade.

For each type of moving average, the period stands for a specific increment in time. Large increments often result in durable, strong breakouts. When using moving averages in swing trading, you must ensure that you do not sell too early or too late. Selling your positions too early may rob you of potential profits while doing this when it's too late puts you at risk of losing more profit in case the trend reverses. One rule in this strategy is that you should sell only when the price of the stock is a little bit lower than the line of the average of the short-term. Most swing trading platforms will calculate moving averages on your behalf. Although this is good, you must endeavor to know how the averages are calculated to be able to understand the changes in stock prices.

Chart : Death Cross

Chart: Golden Cross

How to Apply Swing Trading Strategies to Your Trading

Swing trading is not a new term to most Forex traders. The trading style has been around for years. Most traders have actually done swing trading without knowing it. Anything that is not day trading and not long-term trading can be categorized as swing trading. Swing trading allows you to make the most out of short-term price changes of stocks and commodities. It is one of the best trades because it is characterized by higher reward/risk ratios. The best swing trading strategies are those that enable you to choose the right stocks or commodities to work with. When using the above strategies, you can follow these steps to ensure the success of your trades:

1. Determine the market trend. Every swing trade must be started in line with the major trends on the market. You can use indicators or any other technical tools to identify these

2. Anticipate a pullback. Be on the lookout for potential reversals in the market. This is the best time to trade at a profit. If you trade in the right pullback you will be able to increase your odds and profits.

3. Trade. When it comes to swing trading, you should never be in a hurry to enter or exit a position. Take your time to identify the right trends and price changes before making a purchase or selling your stock.

The type of strategy you choose depends on several factors. First, for any strategy to work, you must choose a type of stock that has constant upward movement. You can follow a number of popular stocks for days to see how the prices will change direction. If the stock's price keeps turning to a downward direction, always feel free to select another one from the many options available. Remember the kind of stock you trade in will determine whether you succeed or fail in swing trading. Besides the type of stock, the market type also plays a big role in determining the swing trading strategy you need to employ. The market can assume the rising trend or the downfall trend. This does not matter since you can make a profit from any of the directions. However, be sure to avoid markets whose prices are not swinging enough. Markets that feature limited or no changes in prices can only give you little or no profit. If you have already entered a position in a stagnant market, wait until the prices start changing before exiting the position. Besides using pre-defined swing trading strategies, you can also customize your own strategy depending on how best you understand the swing market. The first step is in establishing some of the pre-existing strategies and using them as a basis for defining your own trading techniques. For each of these strategies, list down the features and guidelines that seems pleasing to you. You can then combine these features to form a unique strategy that meets all your swing trading needs. To ensure that you end up with an accurate strategy, you must be able to analyze market movements. You may succeed or fail to succeed when using this strategy depending on how effective it is in determining current and future swing trading trends. When trading using the swing method, take time to study daily and weekly charts. As you enter into the market, ensure that these are pointing towards the direction you wish to take. Most people who win in this trade stick to this rule unless trading in options, warrants or Forex using the cycle's theory. When trading over medium or longer terms then you may need to use weekly and monthly charts. Just like the daily charts, you will need to ensure that these charts point towards the direction you want to trade. Breaking any of these rules poses a great risk for your account as you may end up losing your swing capital. Remember, the main reason for using any swing trading strategies is to identify market opportunities that have a potential for success. Every trader that is serious about success must employ at least one of the above techniques in their daily transactions. Just like any other income-generating business, swing trading has certain rules that you must abide by, and using these strategies can help you maintain consistency in observing the trading rules. Swing trading techniques do not work independently. They must be combined with a sound trading plan. A trading plan can be in the form of bullet points or questions. It should contain all the important guidelines or questions that you need to consider before entering buy or sell positions. This may include things such as entry signal information, exit points. You can also include your profit expectations and trading schedule. Most swing trading investors enter short positions each time the market is bearish. They do the opposite for bullish markets. However, skilled traders simply follow the direction and trend of the market to determine when to buy or sell. Like any other trade, you must not allow emotions to cloud your decisions. Some traders have lost huge amounts to Forex trading because of allowing emotions to control them. Inhibiting these is often a struggle as you will find out that some days are hard to get over. As a swing trader, you must always remain calm and accept loses as they come.

CHAPTER 5:

SWING TRADING: PROS AND CONS

This is simply an investment strategy put in place to monitor and make profits from the frequent unstable or irregular short term wavy movements that occur in any well-formed market trend. The concept here is to identify the range and the trend of the market for you to gain profits or reduce losses that happen in the specified ranges. Swing trading is a flexible technique, can be used with equal success in both up and down markets. Therefore if a specific trading range can be established, then the concept can be profitable for the businesses that are moving sideways. The swing trading analogy is a more of opportunistic than realistic because the trader makes an effort to watch or view the trends and therefore will always concentrate so much in the direction of movement of the markets and hence the adage "the trend is your friend".

Swing Trading Overview

Markets do move in waves ever known as swings in the price of instruments. There is no market that will ever move in up trends minus retrace in prices. This is accomplished through the analysis of relevant data. It embarks on the identification of current stock or rather security which rises quickly in price as it further seeks to do so in a very short period of time. It such type of methodology the rests upon a certain sweet spot, which is in between the swing trader and the buy and hold position trader. Swing trading by far is a fashionable way of trading financial markets. It is common with any kind of business strategy to have its merits and demerits. So it is with swing trading. Active traders often make groups of two camps. Swing traders and the day traders. All of them seek to make profits as a result of the frequencies in the short term movements in stock as compared to the long term-reserves. We will be able to explore the pros and cons on both sides then we come up with a conclusive summary of the two sides. Pros and cons of day trader

Pros

Day trading form the name itself entails the act of making several trades in a single given day. This is based on the notion of technical analysis and similarly sophisticated charting systems. The main traders' agenda for the day is making a living out of the trading of stocks, commodities, and currencies. As he makes little returns from various trades and lowers the losses on nonproductive trades. There are no positions maintained or even have non in a nights' time.

Potential in Generating Considerable Returns

The most encouraging factor for the trader of a day is that skill of predicting returns. This could come to pass for the person or trader who bears significant characteristics like being decisive, disciplined with carefulness needed in order for him to be a success as a day's trader.

Self Employment

As a day trader, you control yourself. You are your own driver and decision, so independent of the notion of company business. You could be so supple enough in your operation program. You can have some time off when a need is and work at your best times as opposed to anyone on company level.

No Idleness

All along, day traders fancy most the notion of loving to use their minds in the market settings with other professionals on a daily basis. The unnecessary rush from hipped trading is one thing which not all may admit Yet it is a great issue in their minds to create a life in the business as it could be for the daytime trader aspects or reducing the office workers by retrenchment.

Little Knowledge Required

In many financial related business organizations, posing with the correct or necessary qualifications from a recognized institution or university is a requirement for one to have an interview. As opposed to that, day trading does not require such kind of expensive education from any form of university or school. As much as there are no formal education requirements, however, courses for technical analysis and computer trading skills are key and very helpful.

Cons

Risk of potential loses.

Many people arrive at the profit levels even though the markets warn that the day traders must risk a small amount of money which is affordable via small trades even the initial investment leased by friends. The loses might put them in a days' trade fix, and even an everlasting debt.

Issue of Major Start-Ups and Continuing Costs

Day traders are exposed to a very high completion with the high geared traders, hedge funds as well as skilled business people who invest large sums of money so as to make deals in the various businesses. In such surroundings, a day seller or buyer has got limited choices to decide from another spending largely on trade podiums, modern computers, as good as charting programs and similar material. Other trending or continuing expenses include those costs required for the acquisition of live price quotes and perhaps commission costs which add up as a result of the big sizes of the businesses done.

Your Own Boss Factor

To really make a hit at it, one has to quit his day business or job and give up your steady monthly pay slip. After that, the trader exclusively leans upon his personal knowledge and ability in order to create much return from a days' trader for survival. It is so risk bound to leave your business to a third party and expect to have a similar heavy return from the days' trade. The business may turn to someone else and lose it all.

High stress and risk of wear out

As well you now know that day trading is very stressful basing on the fact that you have to watch multiple screens in order to mark the trade's chances hence respond as fast as possible to explicitly make use of them resourcefully. This is supposed to be conducted on each day and the prerequisite is a high concentration level and also being focused thus, in the long run, can lead to burnout.

Pros or Advantages of Swing Trading

Swing trading lets you take credit of the ebb as well as the flow of markets. As you are familiar with financial markets, they never move In a common direction ever, and if you can take advantage of that situation, you are capable of making more profits or money as the markets move higher above in the few days to come, and also make money as the market pulls back as it may either do sooner or as time goes by.

By virtue of being intermittent

You are able to identify more market opportunities by your irregular frequencies of in and out of the market. Considering any financial chart, you will find out that, there is almost if not always an unambiguous long-term-trend, yet the market could not always be at the support or even the resistance area at all costs. By the irregular frequency of being in and out of the market, you may realize profits; hence identify other alternative markets being set up for business trades. This will, therefore, in turn, allow you to spread risks around and about and locks up more-less capital instead of frequently having to generate margins for new positions whenever you come across a new trade. As you close your first position, it is not so necessary to deposit any more funds in your account in the name of covering the second one. The stop losses are always smaller as may be compared to longer-term trades. Stop losses as far as swing trading is concerned, could be as much as 100 pips as much as a four-hour chart is concerned, whereas a stop loss says on the weekly chart, based on an overall trend could yield to 400 pips as well. In this case, you have a great opportunity of placing larger sized positions other than extensively lower leveraged ones through the longer-term trends. There are clear cut boundaries. The swing trader in, this case, is a highly technical trader. For this reason, he will always have a specific area which gives them an indication of the trade is working against them. This being a strong reason to consider, you should know exactly when it is in not working for you and can, therefore, limit the damage that could arise as a result of the bad trade. In addition, longer-term traders usually are obligated to provide a wide berth into the markets as they still wait for the same to go with the fundamentals. Swing trading in its context is a technical business and based greatly upon searching for a very short trend where the value of the stocks increases very fast. In reference to the Forex Guy "2014," the swing trading time frames give you room to focus best on the market movement as it identifies the trend movement so easily. It just takes a few minutes to get the bias that you are on in a swing trading time frame. You do not need to traverse a variety of data areas for instance company balance sheets as well as other issues in order to obtain the relevant information to hit trade. The narrow focus helps you to concentrate on some areas that will become nice to you in the long run. When swing trading, the main focus is generally on the price and trends. As well, this fact tends to make the trading a lot less cumbersome as compared to short term trading styles like day trading.

You can easily predict your results quickly

Swing trading does involve trades which are over within a few days up till a month. You are able to tell how successful your strategy has been several times in not more than a week. It gives you the ability to be able to frequently tweak your 'swing trading strategy' till you get it on the point where it is most often earning you money.

Generates monthly income

Now that you don't have to stay about for months or years, says long term investment, you will be able to tell precisely the amount of money you made on your trades and how much of the same you can create out of your investment account in terms of income. You may maximize the amount you are earning as you do as few as 3-5 trades in one week typically are made and accomplished in less than 10 days.

Time Savior

It is a type of trading which doesn't have to be constantly searched so it is a deal for investors who don't have too much time, like the ones that trade on a part-time level as you hold on another full-time job. As long as some you become proficient in technical analysis, and still in line with the narrow focus of things which you are looking at concerning a stock, then it won't take much time to identify the relevant trends as you make your trades.

Ease of Risk control

Swing trading has a great advantage in risk management. It has the capacity to reduce risk factors. This is according to Lewis "2011", (stop losses are normally smaller as compared to the long term trades.) this gives you room to place greater sized positions instead of tremendously low leveraged ones through the long term trades). The other factor in risk reduction is that you normally make only 3-5 trades in a given week so that you do not necessarily have it in a broad spectrum of investments to confirm on. It enables you to maintain a very close track of your trades that require only a small amount of time.

Does Not Have to be a Block Job

Anybody who has the knowledge and has capital plus interest can attempt swing trading. As a result of longer time frames. It could be from a week to various days and from hours to minutes like that. There is no need for constant trade monitoring. As a swing trader, you can have more than one business to run that could even take up most of your precious time.

Can Make Many Profits

Every trading opportunity needs concentration. Maintaining trade is not easy. This, therefore, calls for commitment and sacrifice in order to realize more returns.

There is Limited Monitoring

A swing trader could easily lose the business. Whereas there is stop risk, it is even greater and much better than continuously laying your focus on a days' trade.

Not Stressful at All

The fact that this business does not take much of your day's time, there are limited chances of being used up as a result of constant worry. Most swing traders do have regular jobs that occupy most of their days' time which serves as an alternative way of getting or making a living from which they can be able to counterbalance or take care of their bad returns.

There is No Prior Expensive Investment

Swing trading is a type of trading that only requires limited resources in terms of initial investment prior to the business itself. With just a little as the state of the art computer in the house or office with some conventional trading tools, then you will be good to go. It doesn't need any state of the art technology day trading aspect. Therefore this type of business does not need any laid strategies. Since it can easily be done by all willing members and ready to invest as far as the terms and conditions require, we could say that it is a feasible choice. Especially those who are willing to spare themselves for other holdings or business-related issues Swing traders must also be able to explicitly dissipate an amalgamation of fundamental as well as a thorough review of it other than procedural study alone.

Limiting Factors of the Trade

There are quite a number of demerits that the swing traders encounter frequently as they move on with their businesses. They are as follows. As a swing trader, you can easily be whipsawed once or quite often. As the nature of markets, showing support or even showing some resistance at specific areas should not signify that they will in respect of it today.

Basing on this concept, whenever you place your trade, you will be sure that you are risking your funds. This happens quite often than not. The challenge here is that, you will encounter losses frequently however smart you may be. There is a great need for being knowledgeable in technical analysis. It may not be basically a disadvantage, but it calls for extra work. Actually, almost anyone in the market is able to tell the trend on a chart right away from the left to the upper right over a given period of time. However, someone attempting to swing trade, that particular chart, must at first identify the entry and the exit points. This is a concept which only technical analysis can do, however, you need to learn it at first for it take quite some time for you to be well versed with it. It takes a unique mindset as compared to longer-term trade and it is tedious. We cannot say that swing trading is scalping, just that the swing trader will run a risk of being spooked out of the market. In relation to this concept, this could be a psychological problem that many traders eventually tend to deal with in their career. Markets can be dramatic in nature. They can make very disgusting moves overnight while you are asleep and then the market is closed. Suppose this happens yet the market is against your trade, you could wake up on a rude awakening call as you look at your position the next day. Placing stops do not ever protect you against that.

Higher margin needed

Swing trading involves at least an overnight holding of positions. Therefore, high margin requirements are required. The value of leverage is twice ones' capital investment.

There is a high risk of substantial losses.

Just like any other trading style, swing trading is no exception. The fact that swing traders hold for long their positions as compare to the traders of the day, they as well suffer a great danger of superior negatives. These two types of trading have various advantages and also have drawbacks. In addition, you can never say that this plan is more superior compared to the other and hence business partners have a choice to make depending on the factors affecting every trading strategy.

Why Swing trade?

It is in Swing trading strategy that the entire focus is laid upon taking of little profits from the short-lived trend. This leads to a subsequent reduction or eradication of losses at a faster rate. However the gain might not be that much, but it's done consistently over a period of time which at last could compound into large returns annually. Swing trading positions, in this case, can be, conducted in a number of days to a week or months.

Swing-Trading-Strategy

Swing trading strategy takes us back to the basics of swing trading. Other than targeting 20 percent to 25 percent profits for most of the stocks you are trading in, therefore the profit goal is more reserved 10 percent to, or even as simple as 5 percent in the tougher market. These types of increase may not seem to be the life-shifting rewards specifically sought in the stock market, although this is the place where a factor of time comes into existence. Although you still have to factor in losses. Limited gains can only give out more growth in your portfolio only if losses are put to minimal. As opposed to the usual 7 percent to 8 percent stop losses, take the losses at a quicker maximum of 2-3 percent. This could maintain you at 3:1 profit-loss ratio, a most pro-found portfolio management rules for excellence. This could be a critical aspect of the whole system now that an outsized loss could quickly erase great progress made with smaller gains. Swing trades are capable of delivering large gains from individual trades. A relevant stock may dissipate enough strength initially which can be held for greater gains, or even partial gains could be obtained as you give the remaining position to run. Day trading is meant for traders looking for quick generation of returns. Suppose a certain trader risks 0.5% of her capital on each trade. If he loses then he will have lost 0.5%, but if he gains, he will have gained 1% in the ratio of 2:1 as the reward risk ratio. In addition, suppose he wins 50% of his trades if, at all he makes 6 trades each day, on average, he will be increasing it to about 1.5% of his account balance each very day minus the trading fee. Making as much as 1% per day would be able to grow his trading account by over 200% in a period of 1 year uncompounded. On the other side, whereas the numbers look like they are easy to reproduce for big returns, nothing is usually very easy. It's just an assumption. Creating more as much as twice on winners like you lost on losers as you also gain on 50% of the general trades that you partake of usually does not come by very easily. It is so easy to come up with quick gains, yet you could still but rapidly clear your trading account via day trading. Swing trading, in this case, amasses gains and s more slowly than day trading. You can still hold on certain swing trades which very quickly amount to returns in huge gains or losses. Assuming that a swing trader applies the same risk management technique and places 0.5% of his capital on each trade with an objective of trying to achieve to make 1-2% on his winning trades. Assume therefore that he earns 1.5% total on average for all winning trades, thus losing 0.5% on all the losing trades. He makes up to 6 trades every month and as well wins up to 50% of each trade. Now in one month of real business, a swing trader may make 3% of his financial credit fewer fees. Over a period of say 1 year, it amounts to up to 36% which in return sounds happy although it offers limited potential as compared to a day traders' possible earnings. All these example scenarios are meant to portray the difference between the two distinct trading platforms. Tempering with the percentages of the trades having been won, the average win as compared to the average loss, or rather the number of trades can relatively affect a strategy gaining prospect. Now being the general rule, day trading realizes most profit potential at least even on small accounts. Whenever the size of the account moves upwards, it also becomes even difficult or even harder to effectively use all the investment on very short term trades.

Conclusion

Capital needs vary or change based on the markets in question. Day trading, as well as swing traders, could start the businesses with varying amounts of initial investments or capital, in this case, depending on if they trade futures market, stock or Forex. Day trading stocks in the United States may require up to an account balance of $25,000. There is no legal minimum existing to swing trade stocks, however, a specific swing trader will, fortunately, wish to have at least account holding $10,000, and even as high as $20,000 if he is aiming at drawing of an income from the trading. When you do business on Forex-markets nowadays, you do not need any particular or specific amount to start with. Instead, it is a prerequisite for traders to begin with at least an amount not less than $500 or 1,000% more preferably or even greater than that. For one to swing trade Forex, the minimum amount recommended is about $1,500 or even greater than that. With this amount on board, you may be allowed to enter a limited number of trades at ago. In the current market, futures begin with $5,000-$7,500. Even much more capital will be highly recommended. The amounts basically rely on the futures contracts that are being traded. In the case of days trading, trading some contracts would need more capital investment while just a few contracts like the micro contracts may be in need of less than that. In order to swing trade a diversity of futures contracts, you will be required to have at least $10,000 and above of up to but not limited to $20,000. The total amount required will always depend upon the margin needs of the very specific contract that is currently being traded.

There Is a Difference in Trading Times

Both day and the swing trading strategies require time although day trading specifically needs more time as compared to the swing trading. Day traders usually take up their trades of up to but not limited to two hours a day. When we combine the time of preparation, and perhaps a chart or trading review, it calls for more time, being spent at least 3-4 hours, at the computer, on a minimum level each day. Whenever a day trader opts or presumes to work or even trade for more than two hours per day the time investment moves up at a considerable interval and it thus becomes a fulltime job. Swing trading, in other words, utilizes less time.

Time, Focus and Practice

Both swing trading and day trading need a significant deal of work as well as knowledge in order to make profits regularly. Even though, the knowledge needed is not necessarily the book knowledge. All outperforming outcomes as a result of finding a strategy which produces an edge or even a profit after a significant level of trades, and hence executing the same strategy repeatedly.

CHAPTER 6:
SWING TRADING USING TECHNICAL ANALYSIS

Technical analysis refers to the use of charts and other visual imagery to help you come up with a decision in the market. There are many charts that you can use in Swing trading, and that is our focus in this chapter.

Why Is Technical Analysis so Vital?

For you to participate in the financial markets, you need to have some mastery of technical analysis. Remember that many decisions in the market are based on the forecast of the market, whether you are a short term or long term trader. Forecasting the price of a stock is one of the most important steps in making decisions. You can use the charts by themselves or use them in line with other techniques such as fundamental analysis.

Market Timing

Once you come up with the best method to forecast the prices, the next step is to perform market timing. This is basically the right time to enter or exit a trade. When you look at it critically, timing means a lot in the stock market, and the good thing is that you can decide when to enter or leave the market using a few technical tools.

What is Technical analysis?

Now that we understand how vital technical analysis is in swing trading, the next step is to know exactly what it means. The technical philosophy believes that all the factors that affect the market price show up in one way or another in the price movement, which can be upward or downward. Any chart action tells the analyst that something will happen soon, and will make it easy for the analyst to determine what happens next.

Charts Tell You about Trends

In swing trading, you are more interested in what is happening in the market – the direction of the trend and how it affects the price. You then make a decision based on what you see – whether to enter a trade, hold on a bit or exit the trade. Trends define markets. The major use of the price charts is to reveal the existence of a trend and then allow you to study the trends deeply. Many of the techniques that are used by analysts are to identify a significant trend and then determine how the trend moves, and whether they will change direction or not.

The Types of Charts

Many technical analysts use the daily bar-charts that have different bars representing a day of trading. Another popular type of chart is the Japanese candlestick. You can also use line charts to identify patterns and trends. These charts can monitor trends from a few minutes to years, depending on your strategy. The major premise of using technical analysis is that trends exist in the market and these trends persist for a long time. Trends are usually characterized by the formation of peaks and troughs. When the peaks and troughs are rising, it is termed an uptrend, and when the peaks and troughs are descending, it shows a downtrend. These trends can be major, secondary or minor. Major trends last for at least a year, secondary trends for between one and three months and minor trends last for a few weeks or less.

Support and Resistance

You will have to understand what it means by support and resistance for you to make any sense of technical analysts. Support refers to the level that occurs below the market whereby the buying pressure is more than the selling pressure and as such a decline had to be halted. On the other hand, resistance is the level that occurs above the market whereby the selling pressure is more than the buying pressure. To make use of the support and resistance points, you need to understand what a trend line means and what it does. The trend line refers to a straight line that connects successive peaks, descending or ascending. When the trend line is drawn up and to the right, it is called an uptrend line, and when the trend line is drawn down and to the left, it is called a down trend line. The uptrend line is drawn in a way that all of the price action occurs above the line. On the other hand, the downtrend line is drawn in such a way that the price action occurs below the trend line. You need at least two points to draw a trend line, but you need a third line to identify the trend line as a valid one. Trend lines have a few uses – one, they allow you to identify links which you can use to enter new positions. The rule of thumb is that the longer the trend line is and the more persistent it has become the more significant it becomes to your decision making the process.

Price Continuation and Reversal Patterns

Using technical analysis tells you a lot about the point at which the price will reverse or a trend will continue. The presence of price patterns gives you the chance to predict the outcome of a trend. The patterns show the struggle that occurs between the forces of demand and supply and allow you to decide which side is winning so that you can make a decision. Price patterns come in two forms – continuation and reversal. Reversal patterns tell you that the trend is changing direction at any time, while a continuation pattern tells you that the existing trend will still go as expected. Reversal patterns usually take a longer time to form as compared to continuation patterns. Let us look at the different patterns in these categories:

Reversal Patterns

These signal reversal of an existing trend.

The shoulders and the Head

This is one of the most reliable patterns that signal a reversal. The top part of the head and shoulders is shown by 3 market peaks that have been confirmed. It is called the head and shoulders because the center climax is usually raised compared to the adjacent cliffs, which add up to a shoulder. There is a line joining the two reaction lows forms the trend line. If the price closes below the neckline, the pattern completes and it shows a vital market reversal. You can measure the targets and price objectives by determining the shapes of the patterns. When it is a top head and shoulder, you can measure the distance between the highest point and the lowest end.

Double & Triple Tops & Bottoms

Another reversal pattern is the triple top & triple bottom. It is the same as the head as well as the shoulders with the only difference being that the peaks and troughs occur nearly at the same level. Double tops (M's) and double bottoms (W's) have two peaks as oppose to three that are seen with triple tops. This show a reversal especially when the second peak fails to move beyond the first peak, the strength of the trend depends on how the peak moves.

Saucers and Spikes

These two aren't as common as the other patterns, but they contribute to the decision you make. The spike top shows a sudden reversal in trend. The differences between this pattern and others in technical analysis are that they don't have a transition period. The pattern shows a sudden change in working without any warning at all. On the other hand, the saucer shows a slow reversal in trend and is mostly seen at the bottom of the trend. It usually shows a gradual change in the trend. The trend resembles a round bottom or a saucer.

Continuation Patterns

This shows the continuation of a trend, which means that the trend will move in the same direction for a certain period.

Triangles

These show a continuation of a certain trend and they form a reliable continuation pattern. These come in three forms – symmetrical triangles, ascending and descending. These patterns usually show a pause in the prevailing trend before the trend continues.

Symmetrical Triangles

Here, two trend lines converge and meet at a central point. The upper line declines while the lower lone rises. This triangle describes a situation whereby the buying and selling pressures have balanced. Due to this the pattern only resolves when the pattern reaches a breakout.

Ascending Triangles

This forms when a flat and the uppermost level and another upcoming low-line converge. The pattern occurs when the buyers are much more aggressive than the sellers.

Triangle with a Descending Character

This forms from flattened low lines and declining uppermost lines. This happens when the sellers in the market are more aggressive than buyers in the market. All the measuring techniques for the triangles are similar. You need to measure the triangle height at the widest point and then measure the distance from the point at which the trend line breaks. While the symmetrical triangle is neutral, the other two have some sort of bias.

Flags and Pennants

These two patterns form pauses in trends. They usually occur during dynamic market trends. The two patterns are usually preceded by a price move that is steep in nature. The two patterns are named according to the way they look.

CHAPTER 7:
SWING TRADING USING CANDLESTICKS CHARTS

Overview

In our other lessons, we identified that however much greater you are at cross-analysis, the greater the chances of getting up with swing trade. We looked at two examples of analyzing concepts thus the trend-line and perhaps the sustain versus confrontation. We concentrated also on how the price patterns were trending such as ascending and descending triangles , how they were being created b combining the trend-line with support as well as resistance levels. For instance, if you could recall these patterns, then you will be able to create high opportunity, versus low-risk swing trading strategies with marvelous profits prospective. Through the whole course, we have tried to lay the basis of the entire system which functions at the notion of numerous forecasts. Therefore a swing trading plan which intends to start up trades whenever lots of trade and chart communication do come in line with each other. As soon as these good trade opportunities come up, they always result in unimagined profitable swing trades. I believe now you are ready to explore everything that you require or is required of you to know concerning major aspects that are involved in the scheme of numerous deliverables ever referred to as "candlesticks".

Candlesticks

Candlesticks are commonly known as anticipatory indicators. If you have never come across this terminology before, then you have nothing to worry at all. You are at the right place. I am here to help take you through all concepts of candlesticks or anticipatory indicators to the fullest of your understanding and appreciation. An anticipatory indicator gives a signal at a glance of what happens in other markets. Just to emphasize on this point, it is the most important indicator of the markets' activity. Momentum indicators especially RSI or stochastic are as well anticipatory in nature since the momentum usually comes before price. When both of them, thus the candlesticks as well as the indicators such as stochastic relay the similar information that is, therefore, more correctly forecasting what could come up for the very stock. Otherwise, the division or separation or change in the averages is what is referred to as confirmation indicator. Now based on whatever the trading method that you wish to choose, you may be willing to work the available blocking alarm. However, suppose you preferred to be watchful and as well seek more proof, now that candlesticks require a great opportunity of the drift, that is supposed to slightly hold you on a watchful indicator that a turnaround should be coming up.

Reading Bar Charts and Candlestick

Charts Candlesticks are meant to reveal or explain charts for any instance structure, say a month, or a week, a day. Candles can be made for virtually any period of time depending on whatever you wish to achieve. We will start by exploring the candles designed for one day or days' candles. If you are finding it hard to spot out the differences in bar and candlestick charts, it is as a result of nonexistence in any. If you are so keen and quite observative, you will agree with me that there aren't any differences seen in the two charts. They both contain similar information presented in quite different formats altogether. As you see, all candlestick charts, as well as bar charts and they, do have relatively similar information, thus the low standing for; close & open whereas the high signifying period. We can say that in the candlestick chart, however, there is a change in the names. We can refer to the real body is the very difference found in the close and open. When the stock goes lower beyond the exact amount, we refer that to as the lower shadow. Sometimes the candle is white or even very clear it shows that the trade in the day was promising. Whenever the stock goes down the color of the candle will reveal as colored.

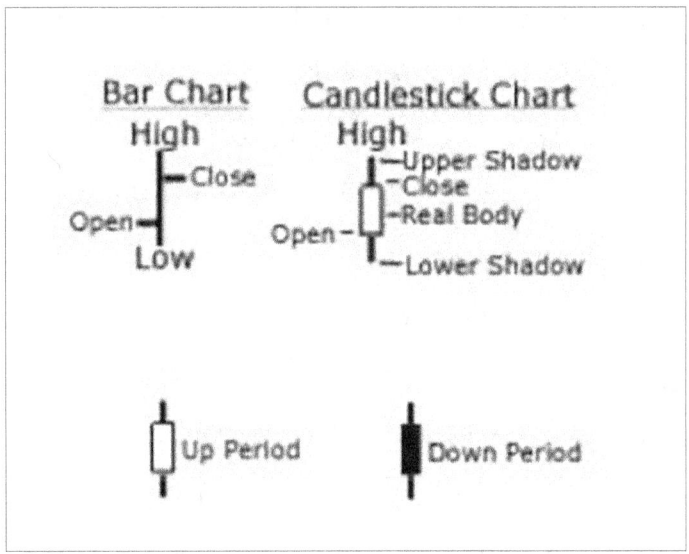

Figure 3: Summary of Candles Movement

The information above explains the concept we have just discussed before.

Think of Candles Innovatively

The information about candles will help you for quite some time if you grasp the concepts well and apply them the way they are supposed to be applied. As much as with other forms of analysis, this information is quite rare for it has not been found anywhere else even with the swing trading concept whatsoever. It has come to an understanding that the amateurs do dominate the market at the opening of the day. However professional traders do close it or they dominate the closure periods. Most of the times, low of the days are mostly set by pessimists. They are the ones who believe that the market was moving in a flow direction and therefore was at the lowest end. The optimists are the ones who determine the high. They are very ready to invest when the prices are still high enough although they weren't correct in their speculation or however much it was a limited time frame. It is quite easy to understand single candlestick. If the above concept is merged with charts, it is then easy to understand and explain them well. We can handle 2 scenarios to bring to light this idea. You might wish to do a personal exploration on your own and at your free time.

Shaven- Bottom-Shave –Head

This type of candle explains a day where the market began at a lower end then it ended up at a high note. This is a day where the armatures were chief pessimists. They posed as the champions of the day by selling earlier. The buyers very eagerly globed their portions. By the end of the day, however, those optimistic people, in the long run, ended the market with a constant rise in the value of the stocks. This is a candle we refer to as bullish, that expects a rise, in the beginning, the following day.

"The Shaved-Head & the Shave-Bottom"

In a relationship with the previous candle, we see that this is the clear opposite of the first position. Whatever is depicted here is a day where the armatures became the optimists. They purchased at the start of the day only to see prices steadily go down. At the end of the trading, prices had moved down drastically and hence the professional pessimists were the ones in full control of the market. This very stock will literally open lower on the next day after showing or indicating such behavior. In most trading seminar over time, we have found out most traders usually draw a lot of sense in candles by understanding them well quite equally. Generally, whenever there are candles that have big networks than the others, you will be obligated to find out on your own whoever was the won the race for the very day, on the other hand, however many other groups of people in the market, including the armatures or the skilled business people. Whenever you ask yourself this question, it will give you an interesting clue of the subsequent trading actions. Candlesticks just like any trading concept have got its merits as well as its demerits that we will want to look at in the next chapter.

Advantages of Candlesticks

As compared to the bar charts, candlesticks have three major advantages.

1. Candlestick charts are very much visually immediately As long as you are familiar with the charting process, you stand at a better chance to be able to analyze and predict the situation after some time not limiting yourself to a day or a month. As with charting, you need to calculate the prices on your own. There are no prior predictions or speculations given for you. You are supposed to be convinced that whatever trend you observed is so because of the shifting in the prices and the changes in the times. It is very possible to clearly

tell whatever happened to stock by just observing the trend within a specified period of time. Candles make it very simple to spot the large range days. They suggest things that are dramatic if they as they come upon a very specific day. A slight change in the range of the day indicates that it could have a slight agreement based on the particular price in the market shares. Suppose I identify a huge collection day, whatever follows is to check or confirm the quantity that the day comes within the return. Assume the amount was not as intended, say fifty percent upper as far as the norm should be, then we can conclude that the range in the large day could, therefore, set the pace for all remaining actions of trade.

2. Vital for spotting reversals Reversals, in this case, are always short-lived in nature. This is the kind that, the swing trader is ever looking for. Whenever we come across the ancient technical analysis talking about reversals, on most occasions it will be referring to formations which happen or emanate over a certain timeframe. The real patterns of reverse are the so-called: "double-top". They are simply termed as shoulders & the head. That is a very short and right definition. Candlesticks, however, are capable of

picking up the changes in the trends accurately as they happen or occur. This is done at the end of every swing markets. Suppose you lay your concentration to all of them, after that they will often sound an alarm to you in an effort to alert you of the looming shifts.

Why Choose Candlesticks

The best description of a chart is the act of exchange involving supply and demand. Whenever there is an increase in the price of a stock, the potential buyers are placed in a very crucial corner. It shows that there is more need by the buyers than the actual stock available for sale. Buyers are interested in getting enough to buy even though the commodity is limited. It also indicates that the potential buyers have the money to pay for the stock at whatever price the sellers have deiced to offer it. Whenever a stock devalues, by deteriorating in the price levels, then we expect that the opposite side will hold much water. Potential Sellers easily get scared. By so doing they may not be willing to go by the current trend on the market. Graphically, the work of candlesticks is to reveal the existing equilibrium connecting the supply with the demand. Sometimes, this supply and demand equation does change. That as well can show on a candle chart.

Second Principle

In general, we cannot be able to make conclusions about candles in a separate way. One key aspect, in this case, is to be patient even if you observed a reversal candle on the market. Patience pays. It is advisable to hold up your breath for more than a day or so that you could come up with a new idea of change. If at any particular time you encounter a candle usually called a Doji, then you will indeed ask for confirmation as of the subsequent act of the last day's trade. Assuming the market's space dwindles down as the rates begin waning, then it most likely good to go for your very same position. In the theory of candlestick, a different group of candles could signal very significant reversals. We will now place our main concentration on 5 candles that caused a general shift in the S andP500 in a period of 6 months. As we explain the varied candlesticks, we will also concentrate on the application of the theory to an elaborate analysis of the S&P 500 chart as we will see below.

Major Reversal Candlesticks

1. Bullish Engulfing

This candlestick is more relevant when it happens or occurs after a prolonged downward movement in the trends. The rate has been shifting so severely, and as such, the prices were meant to drift down harshly. Nonetheless, strong desire and will to acquire more shares definitely come by as it shifts the market by turning things about. The phenomenon earns itself a title. Therefore whenever we talk about a bullish overwhelming candle we mean a representation of a turnaround of the real demand and supply-demand. Supply at a certain time outcompetes the demand but, in this case, buyers as eager as we may compare them with the sellers. Perhaps this could be at the beginning a short cover and more so at the market foot, but as it is mindless of the trend or the shifting, it is more often than not the mechanism which initiates a purchasing charge. When you examine this candle, the confirmation of the size should be relative. Whenever the candle has more potential over the others, it indicates that the reversal will be definite

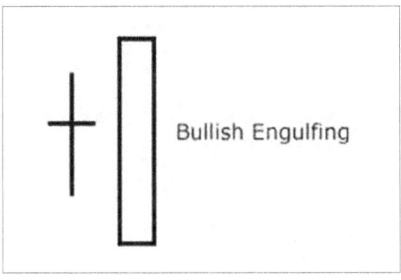

Figure 5: The Bullish-Engulf.

2. The Bearish.

We could refer this to as the reverse of the above discussed engulf. It's quite imperative that there is any form of shifting in the trend upwards, especially when there is overbuying in the market and thus rendered most susceptible to the business owners who are perhaps expecting to get away with good or positive proceeds. Similar options will apply to this current concept. The larger the magnitude, the extra, the change in demand, and the possible supply as triggered.

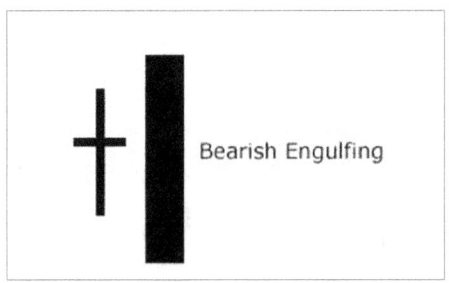

Figure 6: Bearish Engulfing

3. The Hammer

It is indeed a hammer. It marks the reversal which is either of a lower or a quite useful running level. Whenever there is a hammer, there is always a drastic reduction in the prices of stocks. They go far much down to a very low level then they begin shooting up again, thus creating a soft ground even extra, such that they lost it all at whatever time the major sales kicked off. The candle is so suggestive that purchasers have taken up full situation control. All this information can be identified using the pullbacks.

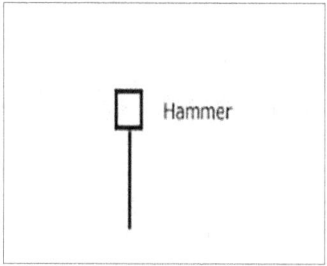

Figure 7: the Hammer

4. Doji

Suppose you were to learn only a single candle, then this could be the most preferred candle that I would recommend would be the Doji candle. A most common Doji as I may refer to it is always cross-shaped. Although it does not bear anybody, it is a stalemate between demand and supply. This is a time whereby a pessimist as well as the optimist; professionals and amateurs all come into agreement. The market equilibrium, in this case, has serious allegations that a strong shift in the upward or the downward trends is in continuity. Anyhow, a Doji as it would appear in a highly explored market or an over-purchased market is thus quite important. Similarly, you may be willing to keenly observe the way the market begins on the following morning to find out on the viability of the market.

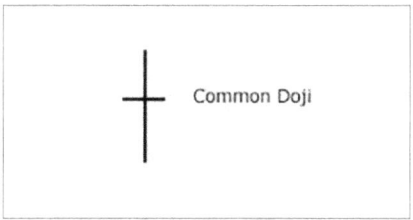

Figure 8: Doji

5. Long Legged Doji

As opposed to the most common Doji, the long-legged Doji does occur less frequent times. It, however, sends out a very clear signal. Thus the market never loved to live at the altitude. Whenever the market is oversold, this candle gives out or sends out a very different message altogether. The day could start on a weak note, whereby purchasers, yet, then is introduced to the market and as a result, it institutes a supply: demand balance by the end of the day. In this case, therefore, the shorts become nervous and try hide, therefore, shifting the market probably in the future.

Figure 9: Long-Legged Doji.

Conclusion

It so surprising the way there is constant repetition in the candles. In the core business of trading in swings, searching for good trade returns, you need to put a lot of emphasis on this subject. Candles when properly evaluated, they are supposed to give you consistent and early warnings of the subsequent changes in the trends. However, you need to understand that there is still quite a lot that you need to learn.

Candlesticks charts are very unique in nature. This is because they provide the trader with such information at a glance:

- Large green or the red candles serve to inform you to up your attention.

- Candles that have small bodies tell you that there are no chances of a dominant force.

- When these two patterns are combined, you come up with, a very strong and powerful swing trading scenario which are very easy to spot. This is a great achievement.

- When charts inform you that institutions are buying or either selling with a predetermined intention, our objective is to meet the acceptable risk

You can also use numerous candles to trade with big funds. It is very common for swing traders to use moving averages for generating ideologies. It is so ok. But considering today's markets, they move very fast. Current traders need to place much of their focus on the hard right edge. Moving averages as the name suggest are so lagging. They remove the noise by merely smoothing out direction although they can be compared to an ocean liner which takes longer to make a turning. Our most updated plan as explained earlier for spotting big money in action is simply focused on candlesticks on the trends of weekly and monthly time frames.

CHAPTER 8:

TREND FOLLOWING IN SWING TRADING

Trend

This is the show of direction using indicators. For example, when the prices are pointing in one direction either the downward or upward movement, that is a trend.

Trend line

These are lines that are visual, drawn under pivot lows or pivot highs that show the direction in which the price of the underlying asset is moving. The trend lines since they are visual, they are a representation of support and resistance in any given time frame. They describe patterns; they show a direction of speed and then also the direction of price during the time the prices swings. The application of trend lines to highs and lows can show or give one a channel. Creation of trend line vary from trader to trader depending on the time period being analyzed and the exact points used.

Trend Following

This is also known as trend trading. Trend following is a trading approach in which a trader buys an asset when its trend price goes up and then sells it when the trending price goes down with an objective of making a profit, with expectations that the price movements will continue. In trend following, gains are captured through the analysis of an underlying asset momentum in any particular direction. Trend trading takes advantage of the market moves. Each time the trend of the market changes, traders will have already strategized on how they are going to trade with the particular trend.

Factors of Trend Following In Swing Trading

Price

Price is among the first rule of trend following. Price is a major concern and the traders must make it a priority too. Traders major concern should be the market price, the current price, what the market is doing right now not an assumption of what the market will do or how it is going to be in the near future. With this in among a trader will be able to choose which trend he wants to follow in his trading endeavors. The current market price is the only price that tells the trader what the market holds.

Money Management

A trader should be able to time the trend well and know when to enter or exit the trade and how much money is involved. Before a trader starts trading he should be able to know how much money he is investing and whether the investment is going to bring him a profit or a loss.

Risk Control

Any trader should be able to minimize risks when entering or exiting the trade. When making an entry in the trade, the trader must put a stop loss when the trade is changing. He should also be keen enough to know the trend of the market before entering the market. This means during downward trends in the markets the trader should always be patient and observe it carefully before making his entry and when the trend picks or reverses in its original direction, he can now make his investments.

Rules

Rules are very important when it comes to trend following or trend trading. Every trader must follow the trend trading rules if he does not want to be subjected to losses. He should be able to know the market price, know the price direction, and know the chart patterns and even the clients as well. If rules are not well followed then the trader is most likely to incur losses because of wrong entry in the trade and wrong exit from the trade.

Diversification

According to researchers, they say that cross-asset diversification is a factor that influences diversification. When there is asset diversification the risk is spread, meaning it is minimized. When a swing trader invests money and earns profits after making a sale and realizes that the market trend is going downward, he can make an exit and invest the money another business-like in options. This diversification minimizes risks and losses are not likely to occur or if they are to occur they will be on a minimal scale.

Indicators of Trend Following In Swing Trading

Indicator

An indicator is something that is regarded as a sign and that thing can show what the situation is like. Trend following indicators is not a surety that you are going to be rich when you enter the trade. There are many factors involved in trade like trading psychology and risk management. However certain trend indicators have been proven beyond a reasonable doubt that when they are rightly followed, a trader is bound to be in business for long making profits. There are different indicators in trend following in swing trading. Below is the discussion of these indicators.

Moving Averages

This is an identifier which gives some support to simulate prices by pointing out the alarms in prices when the prices are taking the downward trend in the market. Moving averages objective as an indicator is to determine the direction of the trend and determination of emerging business lines. Collaborative businesses are very constructive and are able to work by themselves. The Simple Moving Averages –SMA A simple moving average is an arithmetic moving average. It is calculated by adding up all the closing values of overtime, then dividing them with the total number of frequencies of trades. The possible averages that are short will respond more quickly to price swings than long-time averages which are very slow to react on the price changes of the security.

The Simple Moving Average

determines if an assets price will continue with its trend or reverse a bull or bear.

The Formula of Simple Moving Average SMA is

SMA =A1+A2+...+An/n

Where

An= the price of an asset at the period n n=the total number of period

An Exponential Average

This is a renowned weighted mean which places more importance or significance on the weight of the recent prices' information. "The Exponential poignant mean" is also called "the exponentially subjective touching mean". It gives a lot of emphasis on price actions unlike in simple existing mean. The exponential mean responds faster to price changes, unlike the simploe moving averages. The EMA helps one identify trends faster than the SMA. Traders may consider buying when the EMA rises and especially when the stock price goes down near to or lower than the normal level. When the expected norm goes down, investors should consider giving away as soon as the rates dwindle towards or higher than the "EMA".

Whenever the "EMA" shoots, it tends to hold up the rates of achievement as opposed to when the "EMA" dwindles downwards, it provides resistance to the price action. This brings in the attitude of purchasing whenever the rate is near the shifting "EMA" and selling when the price is closer to the falling "EMA."

The Formula of Exponential Moving Average –EMA Work it out

You need to be aware of the "EMA" uses its value as before in its calculation. Newest price data has more impact in moving averages than the previous price data which has just some minimal impact.

$EMA = (K*(C-P)) + P$

Where

C= the current price

P= Previous periods EMA (SMA is used for the first calculations)

E= Exponential smoothing constant.

OR

EMAt= (Vt*(S/1+d)) + EMAy *(1-(S/1+d))

Where

EMAt= EMA today

Vt= Value today

EMAy= EMA yesterday

S= smoothing constant

d= number of days

K or S in from both formulas, which is the smoothing constant, uses the specified number of periods in the moving average.

It applies the required weight to the most recent prices.

Ways to utilize the moving averages

There are different ways of using moving averages. Below is a discussion of the utilization of the moving averages.

Looking at the angles

If you are using the moving averages, you mostly have to look at the angles of the moving average. If they are moving horizontally for quite some time, this means the prices are not moving. The moving average angle lines are above this means there is an uptrend if they are below that means there is a downtrend, though the moving averages do not predict, it only shows the position of the prices.

Crossovers

This is where moving averages are plotted on your chart. A 200-d and 50-d moving averages are plotted on the chart. If a 50-d average crosses above a 200-d average, this signifies a buy. Traders can now buy their securities. When a 50-d average crosses below the 200=d average, a sell signal is established. Traders can sell their securities. These averages need to be altered to fit any traders in his proper time frame. Whenever a price crosses over to a moving mean, it could be considered as a purchase signal and whenever it goes lower than a moving mean, it signifies a sell. Prices are more volatile than moving averages and thus the moving averages are prone to false breaks. On the other hand, moving averages can provide support and resistance.

Moving Average Convergence Divergence

This is a trading indicator that shows the change in direction, momentum, strength and time or duration of a trend of an asset. The MACD oscillator comprises of three series which are collected to calculate it. The three series are the MACD series proper, the signal or average series, and the divergence series which is the difference between the two. The MACD methodology looks at where the MACD lines are on zero in the histogram. When the MACD lines are above zero for quite some time or period, this means the trend is moving upward but when the MACD lines are below zero for some time or duration this only means the trend is downward. Traders who want to buy are advised to buy when the MACD is above zero and the sellers should sell when the MACD is below zero. Since a MACD has two lines, the fast and the slow line, a buy signal is seen when the fast line crosses through and above the slow line, and the sell signal is seen when the slow crosses through and below the fast line.

RSI-Relative Strength Index

As the name suggests, the relative strength index looks at the strength of the prices in the market. RSI views prices as overbought and due for collection when the indicator is above 70 and views prices as oversold and due to bounce when the indicator is below 30. When the prices are up to 70 or above for quite some time or duration, this means the trend is up, but when the prices are at 30 or below, this signifies a downtrend. It is good for traders to buy closer to the oversold condition whenever the price goes up and sell near the overbought when the price is going down. There is no accurate timing or certainty for trend trading in swing trading when it comes to this indicator. In the long term trend of stocks, a buy appears when the RSI moves above 50 then reversing back to it. This means there is a pullback in the prices and the trader can only buy when a pullback has ended and the trend has started taking its original direction. In an uptrend, the Relative Strength Index does not reach 30 in an uptrend that is why the 50 levels are used. When you see an RSI move to 30 or below, this means a major reversal is on the way. When the RSI moves above 50 and back, a short trade signal occurs.

OBV-On Balance Volume

This is a momentum indicator. It looks at the volume in the market to analyze the underlying asset or stock. Granville, the person who coined this strategy believed that when volume increased without affecting prices in the market, there was a likelihood of an upward trend or a downward trend. On Balance, Volume helps predict bearish or bullish outcomes.

The OBV Formula

OBV=OBV prev+{volume, if the close is greater than close previous+0 if close=close prev-Volume if the close is less than the close prev}

Where

OBV=Current on-balance volume ratio

OBV prev=previous on-balance volume

Volume=latest volume trading amount.

Calculation OBV is an accumulation of both the negative and positive volume. OBV shows the total of the volume of the asset in the trade.

There are rules that govern the calculation of OBV, which are;

If the current closing price is higher than yesterdays , Current OBV= previous OBV+todays volume

If today's closing price is lower than yesterdays price, Current OBV=previous OBV-today's volume

If today's closing price is equal to yesterday's closing price,

Current OBV=previous OBV. These rules must be well followed when calculating the OBV in trend trading in swing trading.

The Trend Following/Trading In Swing Trading

We have earlier on looked at swing traders and we know who they are. We have also discussed trend following or trend trading an analyzed the indicators. Since swing trading is shorter and also looks at trends foresee the trends in the market before the investor buys or sells the underlying asset, this means the swing trader is also trend trading. Trend following in swing trading is simply whereby the swing trader looks at the trend of the prices in the markets before he makes his entry or exit. He is there waiting for the right trend to hop on and when it changes in the unwanted or wrong direction, he gets off. When the trend following in swing trading, the trader has to observe the following; If the market is in the right trend, wait for it to pullback to 50MA. This means there is an application of the Relative Strength Index in the detection of the signal. A swing trader must be able to know the strength of the prices in the market before entering. How strong is the trend before he buys or he sells anything? When the trend is above 50, there is a chance that it will have an upward or downward trend. So make your buy at near 50 so as later you will not incur losses when selling. When the market reaches 50MA, wait for a candle. A trader has to be patient and see if the level has stabilized and analyze and know if it will be taking its original trend again before entering the trade. Wait for the candle in your favor. Enter in the next trade if the candle closes in your favor. Swing trading in trend trading requires patience. A swing trader will have to wait until the next trend so that he can trend in order to avoid uncertainties that can cause major losses. Set stop loss in the next entry Since you waited when the candle was in your favor, so in this next candle you have to set a stop loss 2ATR from the entry. This will help you limit your losses and wait as the trend moves to make your profits during the sale. Take profit at a near swing high or low When you have already set a stop loss, be keen on your timing.

Make sure you take advantage of the swings and make your buy or sell and get your profit. In any case, your timing is wrong and you make a sale instead of a buy, you will incur a major loss in this trend trading. Trend following or trading in swing trading it is advisable to enter your trade during pullbacks in upward trends. In downward trends, it is advisable to enter your trade on support and resistance. Trend following in swing trading increases your rate of profitability and cuts down on risks.

Advantages of Trend Followin In Swing Trading

It is Flexible.

Trend trading or following is very flexible when it comes to swinging. A person can move from this trend to another making entry and exit the way he likes according to his chart trend without any restriction whatsoever.

Limited Risks

The risks in the trend following are limited for since a trader is following the trends keenly before making entry or exit, he is not likely to make mistakes that might risk his capital. A trade looks at the volume in the market then goes for the little invest so as to limit the risks in case the trend turns otherwise.

Certainty

Trend trading is following the right trend, hop on it make a profit and getting off when the trend starts going in the downward trend. Trend trading is very predictive. The trend is predicted with certainty before a trader makes an entry or an exit.

Limited Losses

Since it is all about predictability, loses can be predicted if a wrong entry or exit is made, thus the trader avoids any of this circumstance.

Simple to Identify Trends

Reading the trend lines is simple and it does not complex formulas or technical knowledge to do so.

Increases Opportunities

A trader can never miss any opportunity in the market for he is monitoring the trend in the market and is able to know if it is an upward trend or a downward trend and when to enter or to exit.

Lower Cost

The long term trend indicators are cheap cost wise thus there is low cost in use of them while trend trading.

Disadvantages of Trend Trading

Profit uncertainty

Every indicator in trend following cannot clearly establish if the profit duration will be long-lived or short-lived.

False outbreaks

Sometimes the trend can cause a false alarm and make traders invest in the trade only later on to make losses.

Volume sensitive

Trend trading is very sensitive when it comes to volume. Increase in volume of assets in the changes the trend either upward or downward.

Conclusion

In trend following in swing trading, a trader's profitability will depend on how he uses his tools to analyze his trend chart. A trader has to note that an upward trend means the trend is healthy and a buy signal has been communicated while a sell signal is communicated when there is a downward trend. Both swing traders and trend traders use different skills to do their timing but skillful traders can combine the two and do excellently in trade.

CHAPTER 9:

MONEY MANAGEMENT IN SWING TRADING

Money management

This is a technique of budgeting, saving, investing and overseeing the capital usage of a group or an individual. When a swing trader wants to remain in business for long and earn his profit, he must be able to manage his finances well. He should be able to understand how much he is investing and whether it is going to give him, profits, he should be able to know to save some money for emergency situations; he should be to understand how capital is being used in the trade. If his capital is taking longer than the required time or it is going down instead of up, he should have a solution to this; he should know how to manage his capital utilization.

Money Management Instrument

Accounting software

A swing trader must have the accounting software so as to know how to calculate his tax, expenses, income, and automation of billing, recurring payments, credit card processing and even goggle Apps. The accounting software can be quick books or Xero which have gained momentum in the online market.

Budgeting tools

Since money management is a process of budgeting, you need budgeting tools as a swing trader to be able to analyze your income and expenditure so that you do not incur losses. As a swing trader, you must be able to create an outstanding budget that fits your business.

Payroll Management Software

Payroll management is among the hard activities in swing trading. The business is all about timing and if a swing trader decides to concentrate on payrolls alone all by himself, he might end up missing an opportunity to invest. Thus the payroll software like Zen payroll and Benefits helps you as a swing trader to be able to manage your payroll and avoid mistakes like overpaying band incurring losses.

Financial Dashboard

Every trader, not just swing traders must implement a financial dashboard so as to be able to know how healthy his business is. Analysis of your business health is very important because it will help you understand if you are making losses or profits and it will also let you know that if you are making profits how much time are you investing in to get those profits. If you want to manage your finances well you must assess the health of your business.

Cash Flow Analysis

There are tools like float which will help you as a swing trader be able to know your cash flow. Knowing your cash flow helps you decide how much you are going to invest in a trade.

Expense Tracking

You must be able to track your expenses so as to know if you are spending more than needed or it is ok. Knowing how much you are spending will help you manage your finances well and make you be in business as long as you want.

Inventory Management

A swing trader should be able to track his inventory from sale to customer satisfaction, this will help you manage your money well because you will understand that whatever you are selling is what you had invested in and when customers are satisfied, they will definitely come back and increase your sales.

Business Credit Card

It is recommendable for a trader to have a business credit card for this will help him acquire loans and improve his business.

E-Commerce Solution

The world has changed and the internet is everything in business, a trader must have different solutions in the e-market to be able to keep pace and manage his finances well.

Money Management Strategies in Swing Trading

The money management strategies if well implemented will help a trader be able to manage his finances well. Strategies always range from aggressive to passive depending on the focus of the method. The aggressive money management strategy aims at large profits by using greater leverage while the passive strategies aim at capital preservation. The passive strategies are naturally very conservative. Below are money management strategies that a swing trader can employ.

Flat Risk Method

This is the most basic money management strategy. It is also called the constant risk method. This strategy can be used to show the amount of leverage on a trade account at any given time rather on per basis. The flat risk strategy framework varies depending on the capital, the market type, profit objectives and all the risk appetite the trader is willing to pursue. A common flat risk percentage that is used is 1-3%. Calculation of the flat risk strategy is simple, for example, if a trader wants to invest $50000, and the risk tolerance is 2%, then the highest amount to be risked on any trade that he goes in is $1000. The next trades risk value remains a constant of 2%. The result of any trade conducted next after the first one does not change the risk value, for the risk value is constant.

Advantages of Flat Risk Method

- Reduces short time variance

- It is long enough

- It minimizes losses

Disadvantages

- Limits the profits that were to be achieved

- Takes a lot of time to recover the account especially after a long drawdown period.

Kelly Criterion

This is a mathematical formula. According to trading and investment, it aims at defining the probable amount to be risked in any trade according to the assumption or probability of that trades success. Kelly criterion promotes the idea that the higher the risk the higher the return, thus the high probability of the trade success. Calculating Kelly criterion can be a challenge for it is not easy but financial software providers have made software than can readily calculate it for the investors. There are many variations of the formula but most of the traders or investors use the simplified one below:

Kelly%=w-[(w-1)/R]

Where W =% of winning trades

R = average gain of winning trades/average loss of losing trades.

For example If the expected success rate of a trader is 70%, a gain of 7% and a loss of 6%, use the Kelly criterion to calculate:

7-[(1-.7)/(.07./.06)]=.29 or 29%

Advantages of the Kelly Criterion

- Big returns expected because the higher you risk the higher the returns

- There is very little exposure to the trading account

- A trader has the ability to utilize returns on high probability trades

Disadvantages of the Kelly Criterion

- If the loses are to be successive, a disaster will occur and closure of trade will be visible.

- Huge risks because of high probabilities for single traders making it very risky.

- Ability to sustain trading operations because of the size of the account

Martingale Strategy

This strategy is the oldest in the system. Martingale strategy says that the trader takes a precise profit on the win, and then doubles the risk value if he loses. For example If a player has a 50/50 odds and he keeps doubling his value after every loss, this means the player will automatically win the game because the doubled bets cover the small losses. Trading of financial instruments do not exist in simple binary form, it attempts to take advantage of the opportunity present to increase exposure to the risk in an effort to make more profits. Consecutive losses in Martingale are devastating and cause ruin to the player.

Advantages of Martingale Strategy

- Markets provide a high probability of success trades

- Profits are gained in a short period

- Profit targets are precise and profits are quantified

Disadvantages

- When markets trend they can lead to major losses

- Quick multiplication of leverage needed to double

- Huge capitals needed for doubling in case of losses.

The type of money strategy to be employed in any trader depends on the trader's view. Conservative strategies like flat risk may suit some traders while other traders can go for aggressive strategies because they can handle higher risks.

Rules of Money Management in Swing Trading

- Manage your expenses so that they do go so high then your income

- Look at payment options before making a sale or a buy

- Don't think twice about asking for discounts especially when trading with the options

- Before buying your security look at the internet to see the discounts offered

- Do not spend more than a third of your money in payment of debts

How to Manage Money

Budget for All Times

A swing trader should be able to come up with a budget of his income and his spending so as to be able to know what he is expected to do in the business. He will be able to pay his due, know how much he wants to invest, know how much he wants to save and be able to service his long term goals. If a trader does not know how to come up with a budget, he can always seek advice from a certified financial planner. Without a budget, one is bound to spend more than he is earning and this will lead to the business ruin.

Divide Your Expenses

A swing trader should divide his expense and know which are important and urgent and which are not important and urgent. Expenses can be divided into regular and non-discretional expenses and irregular and discretional expenses. Regular and Non-discretional Expenses These are regular and unavoidable expenses but a swing trader should be very keen and be able to control them. These expenses can be grocery, fuel, phone, laundry, domestic help, and entertainment expenses. For instance, one can decide to go and shopping with friends because when you buy so many things you are likely to be discounted.

Irregular and Discretional Expenses

This includes things that are avoidable and needs to be planned for intelligently. The things here may include buying a gold necklace, going for an entertainment trip to another country, buying furniture.

Get the Best Deal

A swing trader must be a good negotiator. He should negotiate enough to get discounts and good prices when making a buy or a sale. This helps save money which can be used to do other things or even buy more assets and earn you good returns. For example, in an attempt to buy an option at $80 the trader negotiates and buys it at $50, this trader is able to buy more and save quite some good amount because of the power of negotiation. During the sale, he already has an upper hand because he bought it cheaply and can still negotiate the selling price and sell at a good profit.

Cost-Benefit

A swing trader should be able to understand how much he is investing and the probable outcome of the investment. If he does not know how much returns he is expecting then he is in the business wrongly for this will lead to his ruin. A trader must calculate the cost-benefit, he must know how much he put in to get the trade running band what should come out as returns to cover the amount that was invested and having more as profit.

Credit Card Advantage

An intelligent trader after the first investment should not continue trading with his money but rather get financing and use the money to trade with. This can be achieved through a transaction with the credit card. The ore a swing trader uses his credit card during his trading the more advantages are there.

- Helps track your expenditure monthly because a list of your expenses is sent to you.

- Extra warranties on items bought by the card which helps you save some money.

- Points are awarded. A trader can redeem these points and be able to get some money for other uses.

- A trader is relieved from carrying cash around which he can do impulse budgeting with or it can even be lost.

- Discounts can be given by a credit card company to the trader, for example, low transaction fee or free transaction for a certain amount for a certain period. The trader takes advantage of this and does more business using the credit card as a payment mode for him to earn more profits.

Benefits of Money Management in Swing Trading

Control

When you manage your finances by budgeting, it saves you the stress of having to run up and down for extra money to do some things in the business. Managing your money allows your money to work for you not the other way round, you work for the money.

Keeps You Focused

When a trader manages or budgets for his money, he is focused on his goals. The goals are well stipulated in the budget and that the allocation to each is clearly outlined, thus a trader can not confuse and do otherwise. When a trader has limited finances, budgeting makes it easier for him to execute his goals.

Shows You the Trend

Money management helps you to know what is going on in the business. You are able to know if the profits have gone down or up by simply looking at the past incomes because you have budgeted for everything that you have done.

Instills Saving Discipline

Money management disciplines one to be able to know how much he is supposed to save, how much he should spend on unavoidable things and how much he can spend on avoidable things. A trader can use the 50/30/20 rule to be able to do this.

Helps in Decision Making

Managing your money helps you make a decision in advance on how your money is going to work for you. Money management helps you know if you are eligible for a debt, more precisely a loan and how much loan can you take and what time is it going to take you to service your loan fully. Enables You Save For Both Expected And Unexpected Costs Money management helps you to be able to save for emergencies like sickness, childbirth, death of a family member and also it helps you be able to execute the things you have planned for like investing this much in a trade at this time.

Helps In Easy Referencing

Managing your money will help a trader be able to look back at his trade in case of any doubt and erase the doubt when he finds a clear picture of the situation. A trader can always refer to the expense and the income, how much he had invested earlier and how much profits he got. Money management will allow him to refer to know the trend of the business in the past.

Helps Avoid Conflicts

When you manage your money there won't be conflicts in a trade-in that you took the money of the stock and invested in options and since now you did not manage your expenses well you don't know how much should come out and go to its original account.

Helps Detect Problems

Money management can act as a problem indicator. For instance, you are able to detect fraud faster if your finances are well organized. You can be able to know that there is extra spending where it is not required and correct it faster before it brings ruin to the business.

Helps You Make More Profit

When there is good management of finances, there is growth in the business and more profits are produced. A trader who manages his finances well is able to re-invest the returns in the same business or another business and make higher returns.

Debt Free

When you manage your money well you will definitely not involve yourself in debts. Money management will make you not go and borrow from friends because you need to improve your business or your life, thus it makes you debt-free.

Plan For The Future

When you manage your money well you are able to plan for the future because everything is budgeted for.

Helps You Balance Between Risk And Profit

Money management helps you be able to balance the risk that you are going to take in order to earn the profits. You cannot all the money you have and invest it without knowing the balance between the risk and the profit.

Makes Sure There Is Investor Confidence

When you manage your finances well, you will have the confidence of investing your money into the chosen trades that you want to venture into. When a buyer wants to buy from you, your financial position which has been brought about by your good management will give the buyer confidence to go into trade with you because the buyer will know that his money is safe.

Boosts Growth

A trader is bound to grow if he manages his finances well for good financial management means more profits which can be re-invested and bring growth to both the traders well being and his business.

CONCLUSION

Money management in swing trading is very important. We have looked at the instruments to be used by swing traders to help them manage money and not spend it on other things. We have also looked at the strategies that swing traders can use in money management.

The flat risk method is conservative and a few traders can use it but some traders can go for the aggressive strategies. In our discussion, we have discussed how a swing trader can manage his finances and the benefits attached to this financial management.

Money management is very important because it helps in major decision making in business. It is very key to understand that for a swing trader to experience growth, he should be able to manage his money well. He should be able to balance the risk and the profit in the trade In money management, there are different tools that one can use and if he cannot he can always look for a certified financial analyst to do it for him at a fee.

In the growing financial technology market, there are so many personal finance apps that can help you with your every aspect of your personal finances.

www.ingramcontent.com/pod-product-compliance
Lightning Source LLC
Chambersburg PA
CBHW070341220526
45467CB00001B/213